P9-BZT-660

WHAT THE **BIBLE** TEACHES ABOUT

MARRIAGE

WHAT THE **BIBLE** TEACHES ABOUT

marriage

Anthony T. Selvaggio

EVANGELICAL PRESS

Preface:
how to use this book

Let me begin by telling you the purpose of this book, its intended audience and why I wrote it. The purpose of this book is *not* to provide you with another 'how to' book on relationships; there are plenty of other books offering that elixir. It is also not a full-length commentary on the Song of Songs. While it will engage in biblical exegesis of various passages in the Song, it is not a verse-by-verse exposition. Its purpose is fourfold:

1. To provide you with a newfound appreciation for the wonders of an oft neglected and misinterpreted portion of God's inerrant and infallible Word;
2. To equip you to comprehend the wisdom which the Song of Songs offers regarding various aspects of romantic love, marriage and human sexuality;
3. To help you begin to think about how this wisdom applies to your own context;
4. To assist you in seeing the glory and richness of divine love revealed in the person and work of Jesus Christ.

This book is primarily intended for couples. Its aim is to serve as a helpful guide for those who are contemplating marriage and for those who are already married. Given this intended audience, pastors who engage in premarital or marital counselling will find this book a helpful tool in guiding couples under their care. It will also function well as a book for study by adult small groups, particularly those groups consisting primarily of married couples. Finally, it may also be used by individual married couples in a self-study format. If, as a couple, you are planning to read this book in this way, I suggest that, separately, you read each chapter, reflect on its contents, complete the study questions and then come together to discuss the substance of the chapter.

I wrote this book because I believe there is a need for it. In my pastorate I engage in a fair amount of premarital counselling. The church which I pastor is adjacent to a college, so I have ample opportunity to encounter many young people who are pondering marriage. Because of this, I began to look for helpful resources in this area. I quickly became dissatisfied with many of the books that I found on the topic of human romance, marriage and sexuality. Many of the books I reviewed disappointed me because they disconnected marriage, sexuality and romance from the Bible. They simply mimicked the shallow, therapeutic, self-help advice offered by the world. Even those books which *did* attempt to apply the Bible to these topics often did so in a 'proof-texting' sort of way. They offered endless isolated lists of verses, some of which had no exegetical connection to marriage at all! Therefore, I decided to write a book on this topic which would avoid both of these errors. This work is an attempt to address the topics of human sexuality, romance and marriage from the Bible with deep theological reflection. My hope is that you will find it helpful in your own relationship as you seek to glorify Christ in your marriage.

Finally, I would like to thank the two greatest loves of my life who serve as the true inspiration for this book. First, I want to praise the Lord Jesus Christ who has made me part of his bride and has shown me the meaning of the greatest love of all. Second, I want to thank my wife Michelle, who is my darling, my dove, my perfect one and my bride.

Anthony T. Selvaggio
College Hill Reformed Presbyterian Church
Beaver Falls, Pennsylvania

knew so that like him you can declare to God, 'Your word is a lamp to my feet and a light for my path,' (Psalm 119:105).

In conclusion, the Song is not a 'how to' manual nor does it exalt human sexuality to the central place of our lives. In other words, neither the Song, nor this book, will save your marriage. Only Jesus Christ can do that. I agree wholeheartedly with the sentiments of Philip H. Eveson who wrote, 'The antidote to immoral premarital relationships and the breaking of marriage vows among professing Christians is not more sex and marriage manuals or counseling sessions but a return to our "first love".'[3] That is the ultimate goal of this book, to help you to see your 'first love' by looking through the lens of human love. With these warnings in mind, we can safely commence our voyage through the Song.

Questions for review and discussion

1. *Discuss how sin has impacted the realm of human relationships and sexuality in our culture. Discuss how sin has impacted this realm in your own context.*
2. *Discuss where you received your instruction about relationships and sexuality. What role did your parents play in this? What role did your church play? What role did the culture play?*
3. *In this chapter we looked at several examples of how sin impacted the marital relationship in the book of Genesis. However, these issues are not just found in Genesis. Therefore, examine the following relationships and discuss how sin impacted them:*

    a. *Samson and Delilah (Judges 16)*
    b. *David and Bathsheba (2 Samuel 11)*
    c. *Solomon and his wives (1 Kings 11:1-8)*
    d. *Ahab and Jezebel (1 Kings 21)*
    e. *Ananias and Sapphira (Acts 5:1-11)*

4. *In James 1:5 God tells us the following: 'If any of you lacks wisdom, he should ask God, who gives generously to all without finding fault, and it will be given to him.' We must all acknowledge that we need God's wisdom to guide us to a proper understanding of human relationships and sexuality. Therefore, as you begin this study pray that God will use it to guide you in your relationship. Pray that he will give you wisdom.*

2. The prerequisites of true love: maturity

*'Daughters of Jerusalem, I charge you by the gazelles
and by the does of the field:
Do not arouse or awaken love until it so desires,'*
(Song 2:7).

The early church father Jerome suggested that the Song of Songs should not be read by anyone under the age of thirty. The great Baptist preacher Charles Spurgeon, although not setting a particular age restriction, also suggested that the Song was not for the spiritually immature, noting that 'Its music belongs to the higher spiritual life, and has no charm in it for unspiritual ears. The Song occupies a sacred enclosure into which none may enter unprepared.'[1] Both Jerome and Spurgeon recognized the same truth — romantic love is meant for those who are prepared and equipped to handle it.

In the next two chapters we will explore from the Song of Songs how young people in the premarital state are to prepare and equip themselves for marriage. It is too often the case that parents, and the church for that matter, have neglected instructing young people about marriage until they are on the verge of entering into it. The Song is a helpful corrective to this all too common error, calling us to teach our young men and women how to prepare themselves for marriage well before the time arrives. While these two chapters are primarily intended for those who are in the premarital state, they should also prove helpful for those who have opportunity to instruct and counsel young people in this stage of life. Although there are many things young people should do as they prepare for marriage, the Song highlights two major prerequisites to true love: maturity and purity. In this chapter we will look at the prerequisite of maturity and in the next chapter we will examine the prerequisite of purity.

The wisdom of the woman

While the Song is primarily focused on the dialogue between the lead characters, there are numerous occasions in the Song when the woman enters into conversation with a group of young unmarried women. For example, in Song 2:7 the woman declares the following to this group of women: 'Daughters of Jerusalem, I charge you by the gazelles and by the does of the field: Do not arouse or awaken love until it so desires.' In this exchange we find the woman teaching these younger unmarried women about love in a manner which is quite similar to the model that Paul commands in the New Testament:

Likewise, teach the older women to be reverent in the way they live, not to be slanderers or addicted to much wine, but to teach what is good. Then they can train the younger women to love their husbands and children, to be self-controlled and pure, to be busy at home, to be kind, and to be subject to their husbands, so that no one will malign the word of God

(Titus 2:3-5).

In Song 2:7 the woman is sharing a piece of wisdom with these young women and she considers this wisdom so important that she repeats it on two other occasions (3:5 and 8:4). What is the meaning of this wisdom? What is she asking these young women to do?

When the woman declares to these young women, 'Do not arouse or awaken love until it so desires' she is telling them not to enter into romantic love imprudently, before they are mature enough to handle it.[2] She is saying that while love is a wonderful gift, it can also become destructive if entered into inappropriately or prematurely. She is warning the young women not to arouse romantic love outside of God's timing. Richard Hess captures the essence of her words of warning in his comments on Song 2:7:

For the Christian, here are the beginnings of a powerful message of physical love as God's gift according to his will and timing. It is not a decision reached by the daughters of Jerusalem (any more than by the sons) but one that must be received when and in the manner that God has decided.[3]

In other words, the woman is instructing young unmarried people to understand that true love must be entered into carefully, at the appropriate time and according to God's plan.

Furthermore, it is important to recognize that the woman is not merely offering casual advice which the young women can either accept or reject, but rather she prefaces her counsel with words of a solemn charge, 'Daughters of Jerusalem, *I charge you*,' (Song 2:7, emphasis mine). The woman is pleading with the young women to adhere to her words of wisdom. In fact, she is calling on them to take a solemn oath to follow her wise advice. She is calling them to swear that they will not pursue romantic love until they are mature and ready for it. However, this message is not just for those young women, it is for every reader of the Song, as Tremper Longman properly notes,

> ...the daughters of Jerusalem are surrogates for the reader. We too are to learn the same lesson: Wait for love to blossom; don't try to stimulate it artificially... She warns the others not to arouse love until they are ready to meet its rigors, both physical and emotional. Love is not a passing fling but rather a demanding and exhausting relationship.[4]

Love is a dangerous thing. It is a sleeping giant that must not be aroused before its time, before we are mature enough to handle its joys and responsibilities.

Perhaps you are wondering, 'Why does the woman issue such a solemn and insistent warning about not rushing into romantic love?' The answer to that question is because she knows that entering into romantic love before one is spiritually and emotionally mature can result in devastating consequences.

26

Let me demonstrate what I mean through two biblical examples.

Samson and Delilah

First, consider the account of the relationship between Samson and Delilah which is described in Judges 16. The Bible tells us that Samson set his eyes upon Delilah and immediately 'fell in love' with her (Judges 16:4). Samson knew nothing of this woman except her beautiful outward physical appearance. He became infatuated with an image. He did not pause to contemplate whether it was wise to become romantically involved with Delilah, instead he fell head over heels for her. He was imprudent with his affections and this had devastating consequences for him and his people because Delilah was working for the enemies of Israel, the Philistines. As Samson failed to exercise maturity in the realm of love he surrendered to Delilah, and the Philistines, the secret of his strength. His lack of both discretion and maturity brought about his downfall and, eventually, his death.

> Love is a dangerous thing. It is a sleeping giant that must not be aroused before ... we are mature enough to handle its joys and responsibilities.

King Solomon

Second, consider the example of King Solomon. He proves you do not have to be young to be immature. Although he is heralded

27

for his perceived wisdom, he displayed great immaturity and imprudence in the area of romantic love. Much like Samson he became enamoured with the physical beauty of women and engaged in impetuous marriages. Again this immaturity had devastating consequences. Even though Solomon knew full well that God had commanded the Israelites not to marry foreign women, he chose to ignore God's commands, displaying an amazing lack of spiritual maturity. Listen to how the Bible describes Solomon's disobedience in 1 Kings 11:1-2:

> King Solomon, however, loved many foreign women besides Pharaoh's daughter — Moabites, Ammonites, Edomites, Sidonians and Hittites. They were from nations about which the LORD had told the Israelites, 'You must not intermarry with them, because they will surely turn your hearts after their gods.' *Nevertheless, Solomon held fast to them in love* (emphasis mine).

Solomon set aside God's commands because he was overwhelmed by immature and inappropriate love, a love which was outside of God's plan and timing. The consequences of his immaturity were devastating for himself and the kingdom of Israel. In 1 Kings 11:4 we learn of the following consequence of Solomon's immaturity: 'As Solomon grew old, his wives turned his heart after other gods, and his heart was not fully devoted to the LORD his God, as the heart of David his father had been.' This failure of a great and wise man like Solomon in the area of love should serve as a stark warning for all of us. As O. Palmer Robertson notes, 'Let all lesser men take note. If the wisest of humans can suffer from romantic illusions, who can presume that he will remain free from temptation and a

28

fall? Beware any romantic inclinations which contradict the orderings of the Word of God.'[5]

Pastoral and personal reflections

As we have seen from these biblical examples, matters of the heart are extremely dangerous. Immature decisions regarding giving away one's heart can result in devastating and often lifelong consequences. I have frequently witnessed these consequences in the context of my pastoral work. I have seen far too many unnecessary broken hearts among young people who gave away their hearts carelessly, prematurely or imprudently. Often these young people become so distraught over these matters that they are unable to focus on their studies, suffer lack of sleep, and enter into extended periods of depression. I have also witnessed those young people who, like Samson, fall in love with an image, only to later feel the sting of discovering the harsh reality which underlies the image. Romance is not a thing to be trifled with and it should not be entered into with imprudence and immaturity. The woman teaches us this very same lesson when she declares, 'Daughters of Jerusalem, I charge you by the gazelles and by the does of the field: Do not arouse or awaken love until it so desires.'

I not only know about the dangers of arousing romantic love too early from my pastoral experience, but I also know about them from personal experience. Let me share with you a brief autobiographical account of which I am not very proud. I preface this account by noting that I was not a Christian during this period of my life.

I first 'fell in love' when I was about fourteen years old. I became involved in an exclusive dating relationship with a girl. I thought I would marry this girl someday. Two years later our relationship ended in a painful way. I was distraught for several months. After this period of mourning and confusion I then 'fell in love' with another girl. Again, I entered into a deep exclusive romantic relationship with this girl. I also thought I would marry this girl someday. Five years later this relationship ended in an even more painful way. Once again both parties of the relationship experienced an extended period of extreme emotional pain. As I look back on those two relationships I realize how unhealthy and unwise they were. Sadly, my personal experience is not idiosyncratic, but rather it is an all too common experience for young people who participate in our modern dating system.

The perils of the modern dating system

While I believe policies regarding courtship and dating are ultimately a household matter, rather than a church matter, I have to question any system that encourages young people to follow the same pattern that I did. I agree with the following comments from Doug Wilson regarding our modern view of dating:

> The modern dating system does not train young people to form a relationship. It trains them to form a *series* of relationships, and further trains them to harden themselves to the break-up of all but the current one.

At the very least, this system is as much a preparation for divorce as it is for marriage. Whenever the other person starts to wear a little thin, you just slip out the back Jack.[6]

Wilson also notes that our modern dating system 'encourages emotional attachments' among young people before they are ready to handle them.[7] He refers to this tendency to allow our young people to become deeply, and repeatedly, emotionally involved with members of the opposite sex at a young age as 'emotional promiscuity'.[8] The church and Christian parents have made a grave mistake by focusing solely on admonishing our young people to preserve their physical virginity while we say nothing about their emotional virginity. Leslie Ludy notes how this type of dualistic message impacted her thinking and actions as a young woman:

> ...I fell under the assumption that as long as I did not *technically* have sex, I was 'doing the right thing' and guarding a sacred gift for my future husband... I was not the only one who adopted this assumption. Many of my Christian friends, like me, thought nothing of carelessly tossing around their heart, emotions, and bodies in relationships with guys — wholeheartedly believing that they were protecting their sacred gift as long as they remained a technical virgin.[9]

Wilson and Ludy both make a point which is very similar to the point made by the woman in Song 2:7 — it is a dangerous thing to engage in deep emotional and romantic attachments without the requisite spiritual maturity. I readily acknowledge that I made this mistake as a young man; I engaged in romantic love before I was ready, and I paid the price. I could have paid an even higher price, but God spared me in his grace. Therefore, I join the woman of the Song of Songs in solemnly admonishing young people not to arouse romantic love before they are ready to handle it.

How to prepare for true love

So how does a young person know when he or she is ready for romantic love? Well, let me begin by saying that it is difficult to provide an exact answer to that question. Reaching a certain age of physical maturity is certainly part of it, but it is not enough. After all, Samson and Solomon were both physically mature, yet still displayed a lack of spiritual maturity by engaging in ill-advised infatuations. There simply is no universal indicator to determine when one is ready to engage in romantic love. This issue must be decided on a case by case basis which is typical for matters of wisdom. However, what is clear and universally applicable is that a person should not engage in romantic love prior to grounding themselves in what the Bible has to say about *how* to

> The church and Christian parents have made a grave mistake by ... admonishing young people to preserve their physical virginity while [saying] nothing about their emotional virginity.

choose a mate and *whom* to choose for a mate. If one doesn't know these basic things then he or she is not ready to arouse romantic love. Therefore, the best way for single Christians to spend their premarital years is by rooting themselves in the biblical principles which will help them navigate successfully the dangerous waters of romantic love.

Let me suggest four things Christians must grasp before they even begin to consider arousing romantic love.

Commit to marrying a Christian

First, a Christian must grasp the necessity of marrying someone who shares his or her faith. This principle is absolutely essential. It is a matter regarding which there can be no compromise. The Bible makes this issue as black and white as possible. For example, Genesis 3:15 teaches us that there are two 'seeds' in this world: the seed of the woman (i.e. believers) and the seed of the serpent (i.e. unbelievers). Genesis 3:15 also tells us that God put 'enmity' between these two seeds; that means there is an inherent antithesis between them. In other words, they are not to be mixed!

The book of Genesis unfolds with the devastating consequences which occur when this command is disregarded. In Genesis 6 we learn that the seed of the woman failed to heed God's command not to marry the seed of the serpent. This chapter reveals that God's people (the 'sons of God') joined themselves to unbelievers ('daughters of men'). This prohibited combination unleashed unprecedented wickedness which ultimately led to severe global consequences:

The Nephilim were on the earth in those days — and also afterward — when the *sons of God* went to the *daughters of men* and had children by them. They were the heroes of old, men of renown. *The LORD saw how great man's wickedness on the earth had become, and that every inclination of the thoughts of his heart was only evil all the time.* The LORD was grieved that he had made man on the earth, and his heart was filled with pain. So the LORD said, *'I will wipe mankind, whom I have created, from the face of the earth — men and animals, and creatures that move along the ground, and birds of the air — for I am grieved that I have made them'*

(Genesis 6:4-7, emphasis mine).

Genesis 6 clearly demonstrates that when the seed of the woman marries the seed of the serpent wickedness and destruction will surely follow.

This passage from Genesis, however, is not the only place in the Bible which teaches this important principle. For example, we saw the negative consequences of becoming romantically involved with unbelievers in the cases of both Samson and Solomon. These two men, by marrying women who did not share their faith, brought disgrace and destruction both to themselves and to their nation. The New Testament also reiterates this principle. For instance, the apostle Paul gives us this very same command when he declares, 'Do not be yoked together with unbelievers. For what do righteousness and wickedness have in common? Or what fellowship can light have with darkness?' (2 Corinthians 6:14). If a Christian has not fully grasped the absolute necessity of this important principle then he or she lacks the requisite maturity to pursue romantic love. Clearly, it is a non-negotiable that a believer should not marry an unbeliever.

Know what to look for

Second, a Christian must also become familiar with the traits and qualities he or she should be looking for in a prospective spouse. Thankfully, the Bible provides us with a great deal of guidance in this area. While the Bible doesn't tell us who to marry specifically, it does tell us who to marry in general; that is, the Bible tells us the type of person we *should* marry and the type of person we *should not* marry. It does this by giving us characteristics which help us to evaluate whether a person is a suitable candidate to be our spouse. In other words, the Bible tells us what to look for and what to avoid. It does this by providing both general and gender-specific guidance. Let's begin by looking at some of the general guidance given in the Bible regarding who to marry and who not to marry.

As we learned in the last section, the most important general characteristic to look for in a potential spouse is whether they share your faith in Jesus Christ. In addition to this vital characteristic, the Scriptures also tell us to marry a person of noble character (Proverbs 12:4 & 31:10) and to avoid a fool (Proverbs 14:7). Proverbs defines a fool as a person who possesses the following characteristics:

1. *A fool does not listen to advice:* 'The way of a fool seems right to him, but a wise man listens to advice,' (Proverbs 12:15) and 'A fool finds no pleasure in understanding but delights in airing his own opinions,' (Proverbs 18:2).

2. *A fool is reckless and lacks self-control:* 'A wise man fears the Lord and shuns evil, but a fool is hotheaded and reckless,' (Proverbs 14:16) and 'A fool gives full vent to his anger, but a wise man keeps himself under control,' (Proverbs 29:11).

3. *A fool is contentious:* 'It is to a man's honour to avoid strife, but every fool is quick to quarrel,' (Proverbs 20:3).

A Christian who has not become familiar with what the Bible has to say on these matters is not ready to pursue romantic love.

Obviously, a Christian should not marry anyone who displays the attributes of a fool. Finally, the Bible tells us to avoid becoming involved with those who are lazy (Proverbs 19:15; 24:30-34 and 26:15), those who lie (Proverbs 6:17) and those who have a 'flattering tongue' (Proverbs 28:23).

In addition to these general characteristics, the Bible also provides gender-specific characteristics to guide Christians in their choice of a spouse. In the chart below I have set out *some* of these gender-specific traits and qualities which men and women should be looking for in prospective mates:[10]

The prerequisites of true love: maturity

Men should look for...	Women should look for...
A woman who displays a desire to voluntarily submit to your loving leadership (Ephesians 5:22; and 1 Peter 3:1).	A man who has the spiritual knowledge, maturity and desire to be the spiritual leader of the home (1 Corinthians 11:3; Ephesians 5:23; and 1 Timothy 3:4-5).
A woman who has the spiritual knowledge, maturity and desire to manage the house and participate in the raising of children (Psalm 128:3; 1 Timothy 5:13-14; and Titus 2:2-4).	A man who treats women with consideration, appreciation and respect (Proverbs 31:28; and 1 Peter 3:7).
A woman who possesses both inner beauty and outward modesty (1 Peter 3:3-5; and 1 Timothy 2:9-10).	A man who exhibits the ability to provide for your temporal needs (1 Timothy 5:8; and Ephesians 5:28).
A woman who is gifted to be a suitable helper and complement to you (Genesis 2:18-24).	A man who understands the importance of self-sacrificial love (Ephesians 5:25).

My point here is that a Christian should not begin searching for a spouse until he or she has searched God's Word to discern the attributes and characteristics of a godly spouse. If a Christian has not become familiar with what the Bible has to say on these matters then he or she is not ready to pursue romantic love.

Know how to look

Third, a Christian must be committed to searching for a spouse in a biblical manner. I think the Bible provides us with a helpful paradigm for this process in the example of how Abraham assisted Isaac in his search for a wife. In Isaac's case, Abraham employed his trusted servant as a surrogate to assist Isaac in finding a wife. Although finding a wife by this means does not apply in today's world, the methodology employed by Abraham's servant remains quite relevant. Abraham's servant did three things:

1. He actively searched for a spouse for Isaac;
2. He prayed to God for success in his search;
3. He evaluated the potential candidate according to God's standards.

First, Abraham's servant began the process by taking active and reasonable steps to find a spouse. In the ancient world, if you wanted to come into contact with a woman you would travel to a well because it was the task of women to draw water. The servant knew this and that's exactly how he proceeded: 'He made the camels kneel down near the *well* outside the town; it was towards evening, *the time the women go out to draw water*,' (Genesis 24:11, emphasis mine). This tells us that it is wholly appropriate for unmarried people to take steps which will make finding a spouse more likely. In the modern world this could include going to a Christian college, church camps and conferences, church singles functions or even Christian-based Internet sites for singles. The point is that a spouse will not just fall into your lap; you must actively search.

38

The prerequisites of true love: maturity

The next step taken by Abraham's servant was to pray to God for success. He sought God's blessing on his efforts. In this action we see the weaving together of the sovereignty of God and the responsibility of man. Isaac's servant prayed as follows:

O LORD, God of my master Abraham, give me success today, and show kindness to my master Abraham. See, I am standing beside this spring, and the daughters of the townspeople are coming out to draw water. May it be that when I say to a girl, 'Please let down your jar that I may have a drink,' and she says, 'Drink, and I'll water your camels too'— let her be the one you have chosen for your servant Isaac. By this I will know that you have shown kindness to my master

(Genesis 24:12-14).

In the midst of his prayer the servant received God's answer. The Bible records this event as follows: 'Before he had finished praying, Rebekah came out with her jar on her shoulder,' (Genesis 24:15). God answered the servant's prayer, and blessed his search, by presenting him with a suitable candidate for Isaac. While it may not always work this quickly, it is imperative that Christians desiring to be married seek God in prayer for a suitable spouse.

The final step Abraham's servant took was to evaluate this potential candidate according to God's standard. He wanted to make sure she was indeed a suitable spouse for Isaac. He evaluated her based on her beauty and purity: 'The girl was very beautiful, a virgin; no man had ever lain with her,' (Genesis 24:16). Although she passed this test, the servant continued in his assessment of her suitability: 'Without saying a word, the man watched her closely to learn whether or not the LORD had made his journey successful,' (Genesis 24:21).

Based on this biblical example, the process of searching for a spouse is relatively simple: take reasonable and logical steps to seek a spouse, pray for God's blessing upon the search, and when a potential candidate is found, evaluate that candidate according to God's standards. Watch them closely to discern whether or not the Lord has made your journey successful.

A word of caution is probably warranted at this point. While Genesis 24 outlines a search process which is relatively simple, it is important to avoid being simplistic regarding the outcome of such a search in our own lives. Genesis 24 provides helpful guidelines for searching, *not* a guaranteed formula for finding a spouse. However, even though this system of searching offers no guarantees, it is a mature and biblically based approach to seeking a spouse. If a Christian is not committed to searching for a spouse in a biblical manner then he or she is not ready to pursue true love.

Seek counsel

After embracing these first three steps, a Christian must be committed to taking one additional step. This final step involves seeking counsel from others. The book of Proverbs reminds us of the following invaluable truth: 'Plans fail for lack of counsel, but with many advisers they succeed,' (Proverbs 15:22). One method a Christian can use to discern whether he or she is ready to pursue romantic love is to seek the advice and counsel of spiritually mature people such as parents, spiritual mentors, teachers, elders and pastors. Here are some suggested questions to ask these wise counsellors:

1. Ask them whether they think you are ready to pursue romantic love;
2. Ask them about their own experiences and mistakes in this area;
3. Ask them about areas in which you need to make improvements; and
4. Ask them their assessment of the candidate that you have in mind.

Do not underestimate how helpful this particular step can be. Remember, God has provided these people to help with decisions just like this. If a Christian has not sought the counsel of others, or if he or she disregards the counsel of others, then that Christian is not ready to pursue romantic love.

Fall in love with Christ first

In summary, young people can begin the process of ascertaining whether they possess the requisite maturity to begin pursuing romantic love by evaluating whether they fully grasp the importance of marrying a believer, the biblical qualifications and characteristics of a godly spouse, the biblical pattern for seeking a spouse, and the wisdom of seeking the counsel of others. Therefore, instead of running around like a headless chicken, searching for romantic love, a young Christian should spend their premarital years learning these things. Christian young people should concern themselves with their true first love: Jesus Christ. They should cultivate the riches of their relationship with him before seeking any other. These premarital years should be spent studying God's Word, growing in Christ and seeking wise counsel in order to prepare for marriage. The unmarried Christian should take the solemn oath which the woman charges them to take, 'Do not arouse or awaken love until it so desires.'

Cultivating spiritual maturity and prudence, however, is just one part of what young people should do in preparation for marriage. The woman's words of wisdom in Song 2:7 not only require the prerequisite of spiritual maturity before seeking true love, but they also issue a call for sexual purity in this stage of life. We'll look at this second prerequisite in the following chapter.

Questions for review and discussion

1. *Contemplate the concept of 'emotional promiscuity' as it was defined in this chapter. Ask yourself if you are engaging in this type of behaviour. If you are in a group setting discuss what you think about this concept and the pros and cons of the modern dating system.*

2. *If you are a parent of a Christian young person, engage in a discussion with your child in order to establish some agreed-upon boundaries and expectations regarding how, and when, you expect your child to search for a spouse. If you are a Christian young person, initiate this type of discussion with your parents.*

3. *Take some time to contemplate the importance of marrying a fellow believer. Begin by reading the following texts which address this issue: Exodus 34:15-16; Deuteronomy 7:3-4; Judges 3:4-6; 1 Kings 11:1-11; Nehemiah 13:23-27; and 2 Corinthians 6:14-18. If you are unmarried, after reading these texts pray to God and vow before him not to marry an unbeliever. Share this commitment with your parents, your pastor and your close friends. If you are in a group setting, discuss these texts and share insights with one another about the dangers of marrying an unbeliever.*

4. *Pause to contemplate the importance of seeking counsel from others about your preparedness for marriage. Read the following texts and meditate on the importance of seeking advice in this area: Proverbs 1:5; 11:14; 12:15; 13:10; 15:22; 19:20; 20:18; and 27:9. If you are in a group setting, discuss these texts and share examples of how God has used wise counsellors to help you in matters of romance.*

5. *Read Ecclesiastes 12 and contemplate its message to you. What does this text call you to do during your youth? What implication does this call have on the timing of your search for a spouse?*

3. The prerequisites of true love: purity

'Daughters of Jerusalem, I charge you by the gazelles and by the does of the field:
Do not arouse or awaken love until it so desires'
(Song 2:7).

Our culture idolizes sex and it beckons us to join in this idolatry. It is constantly thrusting sexual images before our eyes through television, the Internet, billboards, shopping catalogues and even in the storefronts of our shopping malls. Given the ubiquity of these images in our world it is nearly impossible to go through a day without viewing a sexually explicit image. One social commentator has compared the effect of these sexually explicit images to that of second-hand smoke from cigarettes. He refers to it as 'second-hand smut'.[1] We may not desire or choose to be consumers of the smut of our culture, but just like the second-hand smoke from a cigarette we breathe it in every day and it harms us. One of the primary ill effects of second-hand smut is that it encourages our young people to awaken and explore sexual desire before the proper time and outside of the proper context. For example, consider the films which Hollywood markets to teenagers in our culture. These films so often suggest that losing one's virginity is the goal and meaning of life. They depict it as a glorious milestone of adulthood. This message encourages young people to arouse their sexual desires outside of God's parameters. In contrast to our culture's message, the Song of Songs forcefully charges unmarried people *not* to arouse sexual desire outside of God's timing. Whereas our popular culture calls our young people to exercise sexual freedom, promiscuity and perversity, the Song of Songs calls on them to exercise sexual restraint and purity. The Song of Songs tells us that a young person is to prepare for true love by remaining sexually pure. Purity is the second prerequisite of true love.

This call to sexual purity, like the call to maturity, may be found in the woman's charge to the daughters of Jerusalem in Song 2:7. In this verse the woman warns these young unmarried women to 'not arouse or awaken love until it so desires'. She charges those who are unmarried to not only avoid arousing the *emotional* aspects of romantic love prematurely, but also to avoid arousing its *physical* aspects prematurely. Why does she issue this warning?

The woman issues this warning because she recognizes that arousing sexual desire at an inappropriate time, and in an improper context, is not only displeasing to God but it can also result in a devastating impact on the life of a young person and on the lives of those around him or her. Clearly, our own culture displays ample evidence of the devastating impact of arousing sexual desire before its time. The social ills of teen pregnancy, sexually transmitted disease and abortion are all related to awakening sexual desire before its time. Sex was intended to give life, but it can also destroy life if it is aroused inappropriately. This is why the woman issues her solemn charge to 'not arouse or awaken love until it so desires' (Song 2:7).

Her own personal struggle

It is important to recognize that the woman is not offering mere abstract theological platitudes in her warning. Rather, she is speaking from her own personal struggle with this issue. In chapter two of the Song the woman is wrestling with the awakening of her own sexual desire as she approaches marriage. When she voices this powerful charge to the daughters of Jerusalem she is likely betrothed, but not yet married.[2] Therefore, she is experiencing the natural physical desires which begin to develop and foment during this stage of human romance. She is beginning to feel the overwhelming power of sexual desire and temptation. In other words, she is speaking from her own very real experience. She realizes that she is beginning to get ahead of herself sexually. She is beginning to engage in something which is difficult to avoid when two people are this deeply in love: sexual fantasizing. However, the woman also knows that to entertain these fantasies is a dangerous thing in this phase of life. She fully recognizes that sexual desire is a genie which, once released, cannot easily be put back into the bottle. She is aware of the fact that one little

> She fully recognizes that sexual desire is a genie which, once released, cannot easily be put back into the bottle.

spark of sexual desire can turn into a wildfire of uncontrolled lust. Therefore, when she warns the young women to avoid sparking this desire before the appropriate time she is also issuing a reminder and warning to herself. As one commentator notes, 'In speaking to the daughters of Jerusalem, she is speaking to herself. She is basically telling herself to cool it, to wait for the appropriate time. For the Christian the appropriate time is always within marriage, and never outside of it.'[3] It is imperative that young unmarried people heed this personal warning of the woman to avoid arousing sexual desire prematurely. However, the validity of this warning does not rest solely on the personal experience of the woman in the Song of Songs, but rather it can be gleaned from the entire teaching of the Bible.

The biblical pattern of sexual sin

The Bible informs us that sin begins with temptation and evil desire long before it fully blossoms into active transgression. For example, the Epistle of James reveals that sin unfolds as follows: 'but each one is tempted when, by his own evil desire, he is dragged away and enticed. Then, after desire has conceived, it gives birth to sin; and sin, when it is full-grown, gives birth to death,' (James 1:14-15). It is too often the case that unmarried people get involved in relationships which quickly spiral out of control in the area of sexuality. They allow themselves to be entangled in sexual desire and soon this desire overwhelms them and leads them into full-blown sexual sin. Sometimes we make the mistake of thinking that Christians are immune to this type of pattern, but they are not. As Douglas Wilson so aptly put it, 'We somehow think a godly Christian is one who can pre-heat the oven without cooking the roast.'[4] It is all too easy for unmarried people in our culture to rationalize their sin and to convince themselves that they must gratify their lustful desires. In essence, they become seduced by seduction and this leads to devastating results. We see many examples of this dynamic in the Bible. Let's look at two of them.

Amnon and Tamar

In 2 Samuel 13 we learn that David's eldest son Amnon became infatuated with his half-sister Tamar. The Bible states that he 'fell in love' with Tamar (2 Samuel 13:1) and quickly became 'frustrated' by his inability to be with her sexually (2 Samuel 13:2). He then began a process by which he convinced himself that he must have Tamar. This rationalization process led him to turn to his friend Jonadab for assistance. These two men conspired to lure Tamar into Amnon's house by having Amnon feign sickness. After she arrived at the house with some food for her allegedly sick half-brother, Amnon demanded that everyone leave the house except for Tamar. When he had her alone, Amnon then lured Tamar into his bedroom: 'Then Amnon said to Tamar, "Bring the food here into my bedroom so I may eat from your hand"' (v. 10). His sexual fantasizing and planning then climaxed in sinful fruition: 'But when she took it to him to eat, he grabbed her and said, "Come to bed with me, my sister,"' (v. 11). Tamar responded to Amnon's advances by refusing them, but Amnon would not take 'no' for an answer. He was so obsessed with his lust that he proceeded to rape Tamar.

Do you recognize how the pattern of sin articulated in James 1:14-15 unfolds in this account? Amnon began by lusting in his heart for this sexual experience, he actively plotted about it, he orchestrated the circumstances which would allow it to be realized and then he made it happen. The process began with evil desire long before it was consummated in active transgression. This is the common pattern of sexual sin. Sexual fixation leads to sinful fruition. Amnon's fixation on Tamar created an unyielding urge which he convinced himself he had to satisfy at any cost. To put it plainly, he had to have Tamar. But what is truly amazing about this account is that after Amnon satisfied his lusts, after he got what he thought he wanted and needed, he responded to Tamar as follows: 'Then Amnon hated her with intense hatred. In fact, he hated her more than he had loved her. Amnon said to her, "Get up and get out!"' (v. 15). When Amnon finally got the woman he thought he needed to have so badly he rejected her. He told her to 'get out'!

How often have you heard a similar story in our own culture? The story goes something like this. A young man becomes convinced that he must have a certain young woman. He vows to her that he intends to marry her and love her for ever. Then, after engaging in sexual sin with her, he comes to hold her in contempt and rejects her for another young woman. He moves on to his next conquest. Like Amnon, the young man says to the young woman, 'Get up and get out!' Like Tamar, the young woman leaves, sexually violated and emotionally wounded. These are truly devastating results. Sometimes, however, the consequences of sexual sin go far beyond a broken heart and sexual violation. Amnon's story did not end with his rape and rejection of Tamar. Amnon bore further, and even graver, consequences for his sin. After Tamar's brother Absalom learned of the rape of Tamar he determined to kill Amnon and then successfully carried out his plot (2 Samuel 13:28-29). The end result of Amnon's inappropriate arousing of his sexual desire was death.

Reuben and Bilhah

Another biblical example of the devastating impact of lustful thoughts is found in Reuben's sinful affair with Bilhah, his father's concubine (Genesis 35:22). After the death of his mother Rachel, Reuben immediately took advantage of the situation to fulfil his lusts with Bilhah, his mother's closest servant girl. The Bible does not tell us how long Reuben had entertained this lust for Bilhah, but the fact that he fulfilled it immediately after his mother's death suggests that he had been thinking about it for a while. It would have been a violation of ancient Near Eastern mores for him to have sexual relations with his mother's closest servant while his mother was living.[5] Therefore, it is possible that Reuben had this passion brewing within him for some time and simply waited for the opportunity to fulfil it. The consequences of Reuben's uncontrolled sexual desire were immediate, severe and generational.

When Reuben's father Jacob learned of Reuben's actions he punished him by removing his rights as firstborn son. This punishment is recorded in 1 Chronicles 5:1-2:

> The sons of Reuben the firstborn of Israel (he was the firstborn, but when he defiled his father's marriage bed, his rights as firstborn were given to the sons of Joseph son of Israel; so he could not be listed in the genealogical record in accordance with his birthright, and though Judah was the strongest of his brothers and a ruler came from him, the rights of the firstborn belonged to Joseph)...

Reuben's one moment of lust cost him and his descendants dearly. He was transformed from being the favoured firstborn to a mere footnote in the history of redemption. However, there are additional lessons to learn from Reuben's ill-advised awakening of sexual desire.

O. Palmer Robertson explores the cost of Reuben's transgression in his helpful book *The Genesis of Sex*. Robertson notes that as a result of Reuben's lust he earned a 'reputation he could never escape'.[6] As Robertson puts it, 'This one act, presumably done in secret, became the hallmark of his life.'[7] It is important for young people to note that Reuben's case is not ancient history. The same cost is often paid by young people in our own day who allow their sexual desires to overtake them. They engage in one act that earns them a reputation which they cannot escape and which becomes the hallmark of their lives. In addition, Robertson suggests that as a result of his uncontrolled lust Reuben created a circumstance which destined him to 'never excel'.[8] As Robertson points out, 'The subsequent history of Israel proves this point. No prophet, no priest, no judge, no king is ever recorded as having arisen from the tribe of Reuben.'[9] Once again, Reuben's case is not ancient history. Unmarried people who allow their sexual desires to spiral out of control can quickly find themselves facing the very same consequences as Reuben, particularly if their lust leads to children out of wedlock. How many promising young lives have been inextricably altered because of one moment of lust?

The role of parents

The examples of Amnon and Reuben serve as helpful reminders that inappropriate sexual desire can be both deadly and destructive. Therefore, in order to avoid these consequences, young people should prepare themselves for marriage by cultivating their personal chastity and purity during their unmarried years. Young people must personally take upon themselves the solemn charge of the woman not to arouse sexual desire prematurely. However, young unmarried people need help in this

> Young people should prepare themselves for marriage by cultivating their personal chastity and purity during their unmarried years.

53

area and, therefore, it is vital for parents to play an active role in protecting the purity of their children. We see this pattern in the Song of Songs.

In Song 8:8-9 we witness the woman's brothers assisting her with preserving her sexual purity. In this section of the Song we find the brothers filling the role which was typically played by fathers in the ancient world. This suggests that the woman's father was likely deceased and the brothers had stepped into his role. Therefore, as you consider this account it is proper for you to view the brothers as playing the role that parents are intended to play. In these verses the brothers declare: 'We have a young sister, and her breasts are not yet grown. What shall we do for our sister for the day she is spoken for? If she is a wall, we will build towers of silver on her. If she is a door, we will enclose her with panels of cedar.' In these verses the brothers employ two metaphors ('wall' and 'door') to describe the options available to their sister regarding her sexual purity. The verses also detail how the brothers will respond to each of her possible choices. Before we examine the meaning of these metaphors and the possible responses of the brothers, it is important to note that while these particular verses address the chastity of a woman, the principles also apply to young men.

A wall or a door?

The first metaphor used in these verses is that of a 'wall'. The brothers state the following of their sister: 'If she is a *wall*, we will build towers of silver on her,' (emphasis mine). The meaning of this metaphor is not difficult to grasp. A wall is a structure which does not allow access to what is behind it. Therefore, the wall serves as a metaphor for sexual purity. It is a way of saying that she is sexually inaccessible. The brothers indicate that if their sister chooses the path of purity then they will respond by building silver towers, or battlements, on her. This metaphor of building towers and battlements on their sister means that the brothers will reward her choice in favour of purity by helping to reinforce her defences against sexual sin. In other words, if she chooses sexual purity they will be there to assist her in achieving this godly goal.

However, these verses indicate that the woman has another option available to her regarding her sexual purity. Instead of being a wall, she could choose to become a 'door'. The brothers declare, 'If she is a *door*, we will enclose her with panels of cedar,' (emphasis mine). The metaphor of a door is also not difficult to comprehend. A door allows access to what is behind it. Obviously, this is a metaphor for sexual promiscuity. It is a way of saying that she is sexually available.

The brothers imply that if their sister takes the path of promiscuity then they will step in to prevent her from defiling herself by enclosing her with 'panels of cedar'. The imagery here is of boarding up a door to deny access. In fact, the New American Standard Bible uses the word 'barricade' in its translation of this verse. It is also important to point out that cedar wood was known in the ancient world for its strength and durability. In other words, the brothers are serious about protecting the purity of their sister and they will take action to preserve her from sexual sin.

It is important for families, particularly parents, to follow the pattern set forth by the brothers in the Song. Parents should make certain that they encourage and reinforce the purity of children who choose to be like a 'wall' when it comes to their sexual purity. It is also vitally important for parents to correct children who are displaying evidence that they desire to be a 'door' when it comes to their sexual purity. Parents should be watching for the signs which often precede sexual impurity such as deep romantic involvement with a young person of the opposite sex and lack of modesty in dress and behaviour. If parents notice that their child is acting like a door, it is their responsibility to grab the cedar fast! Remember, God has given children to parents as a gift to steward according to his commands. It is true that parents cannot always prevent their children from being sexually unchaste, but when parents see the warning signs they must take action. Permissiveness in parenting in this area can yield dreadful consequences for a child.

The woman's choice

The good news in the Song of Songs is that the woman, with the help of her family, chose the path of purity. She became a 'wall' and not a 'door'. She testifies to this fact in Song 8:10 where she declares, '*I am a wall*, and my breasts are like towers. Thus I have become in his eyes like one bringing contentment,' (emphasis mine). She chose to keep her purity even though she had realized her physical sexual maturity (i.e. 'my breasts are like towers').[10] The result of her choice to preserve her purity was that she found favour in the eyes of her lover, her husband: 'Thus I have become in his eyes like one bringing contentment.'

Therefore, the woman's decision to maintain her purity until marriage resulted in her being more attractive and pleasing to the love of her life. Maintaining sexual purity prior to marriage not only glorifies God, but it also brings glory to the unmarried person who makes this commitment. The woman preserved her purity until the time that God gave her a husband; this is how God intends all unmarried people to live.

Practising purity

As we have seen in this section on purity, entertaining sexual thoughts and desires before marriage is a dangerous, destructive and, sometimes, even deadly game. Young people must keep in mind that Jesus teaches that lustful thoughts are sinful even if they are never acted upon: 'But I tell you that anyone who looks at a woman lustfully has already committed adultery with her in his heart,' (Matthew 5:28). Jesus informs us that the battle for purity begins internally in our hearts and minds. It is waged on the battlefield of our thought life. Therefore, Christian young people must prepare themselves for this battle by purifying their thoughts and seeking God in prayer. They should pray like the psalmist in Psalm 19 who prays, 'May the words of my mouth and the meditation of my heart be pleasing in your sight,' (Psalm 19:14).

> The battle for purity begins internally in our hearts and minds. It is waged on the battlefield of our thought life.

Commentator Tom Gledhill offers the following helpful comments regarding how we are to wage the spiritual war for sexual purity:

> We are all so clever at rationalizing our own desires, at excusing our own lack of self-discipline of our bodies and of our thought-lives. But we need to be ruthless in this matter, as Jesus himself taught.[11] If what we see, touch, feel, read or hear, causes a wrong chain of thought to originate in our minds, then we are to be severe on ourselves, and shut our eyes, and refrain from touching or reading or watching. Not that the desire instincts are wrong in themselves. What is wrong is when those desires run away with us, and spiral totally out of control, and find their fulfillment in illegitimate ways.[12]

Gledhill's advice embodies the substance of the apostle Paul's admonishment in 2 Timothy 2:22: 'Flee the evil desires of youth, and pursue righteousness, faith, love and peace, along with those who call on the Lord out of a pure heart.'

Looking to the pure one

Romantic longing and sexual desire are not inappropriate, nor are they evil in themselves. However, as we have seen in this chapter, these things can have devastating results when engaged in outside of God's prescribed boundaries. The call to maintain sexual purity is clearly a challenging one. Therefore, it is important to remember that the Christian is not alone in this endeavour. Jesus promises to help us to maintain our sexual purity. He has given us his Spirit, his Word, our parents, fellow Christians and his church to guide us and fortify us. He also understands the struggles that accompany temptation. The Bible tells us that Jesus was made just like us, that he understands our weaknesses: 'For we do not have a high priest who is unable to sympathize with our weaknesses, but we have one who has been tempted in every way, just as we are — yet was without sin,' (Hebrews 4:15). Christian young people must not ultimately look to themselves to produce purity, but rather they must look to Jesus for their purity. He is the only pure one. He gives us the strength to remain pure.

Before I bring this chapter to a close, I want to extend a word of encouragement to those who have experienced the pain of sexual sin in their own lives. I want readers in this category to know that Jesus not only helps us to maintain our purity, but he also forgives those who have fallen in this area. If you have confessed and repented of your sin, the good news is that there is forgiveness in Christ (1 John 1:9). He is able to restore you completely through his holiness and righteousness. He restores your purity. Remember, the blood line of Jesus Christ includes people who engaged in gross sexual sin. His blood line includes both a repentant harlot (Rahab) and a repentant adulterer (King David). Also, be encouraged by the fact that during his earthly ministry Jesus particularly reached out to those who had engaged in sexual sin. For example, he ate with prostitutes and gently conversed with a Samaritan woman who was a serial adulterer (John 4). The gospel of Jesus Christ holds out hope of redemption for all people and for all sins. Therefore, all unmarried Christians should place their trust in Jesus Christ for their purity. He alone is able to help the Christian keep the charge of the woman found in Song 2:7 not to 'arouse or awaken love until it so desires'.

Questions for discussion and review

1. *Read the following texts: 2 Samuel 13; Proverbs 4:23; Matthew 5:29-30; 1 Corinthians 6:9-10; 2 Timothy 2:22; and 1 Peter 2:11. Contemplate their bearing on the matter of awakening sexual desire before marriage. If you are presently engaging in fantasizing about sexuality make a commitment to stop this practice. Pray to God for forgiveness and strength. When you are tempted remind yourself of these texts and the power of Christ which can deliver you from the dominion of sin. If you are in a group setting, discuss the practical application of these texts to the area of sexual purity.*

2. *Read the following texts: Romans 13:12-13; 1 Corinthians 5:11; 1 Corinthians 6:13, 18; 2 Corinthians 12:21; Galatians 5:16, 19; Ephesians 5:3-4; 1 Thessalonians 4:3-5, 7; 1 Peter 4:3; Jude 7. What do these texts reveal about a Christian's relationship to sexual immorality? How are Christians to respond to sexual immorality? What are the consequences of engaging in sexual immorality?*

3. *Make a commitment right now to be a 'wall' instead of a 'door' when it comes to sexual purity. Evaluate yourself to see if there are areas of your life which suggest that you are following the path to promiscuity. Are you becoming too emotionally involved with a person of the opposite sex? Are you dressing*

in a manner which suggests that you are sexually available? If you are a young person, do you desire a relationship which is inappropriate for your age level? Are you viewing your parents' efforts to restrict your involvement with the opposite sex in a rebellious manner? If you recognize that you are on the pathway to becoming a 'door' with regard to your sexuality take immediate corrective action to reorient yourself on the path of purity. If you are in a group setting, discuss ways in which parents and the church can encourage young unmarried people to be 'walls' instead of 'doors'.

4. *Read Psalm 1 and think about the advice it gives about what a godly person does and does not do. Contemplate how Psalm 1 applies to the area of sexual purity.*

4. The nature of true love: exclusive

True love

True love is a sacred flame
That burns eternally,
And none can dim its special glow
Or change its destiny.
True love speaks in tender tones
And hears with gentle ear,
True love gives with open heart
And true love conquers fear.
True love makes no harsh demands
It neither rules nor binds,
And true love holds with gentle hands
The hearts that it entwines.

(Helen Steiner Rice)

'Place me like a seal over your heart, like a seal on your arm; for love is as strong as death, its jealousy unyielding as the grave. It burns like blazing fire, like a mighty flame. Many waters cannot quench love; rivers cannot wash it away. If one were to give all the wealth of his house for love, it would be utterly scorned'
(Song of Songs 8:6-7).

True love is an elusive concept. It does not lend itself to a 'scientific' or 'textbook' definition. It is incredibly difficult to articulate the meaning of true love in concrete terms. It is one of those intangible concepts which are best defined by means of poetry. Perhaps that is why many an inspirational poet, such as Helen Steiner Rice, endeavoured to define true love through poetic verse. But we do not have to rely on uninspired poetry to give us a sense of the meaning of true love for the Bible contains its own poetic definition of true love in the Song of Songs. We find that inspired definition in Song of Songs 8:6-7.

Many commentators consider these two verses to be the poetic pinnacle of the entire book. For example, Robert Davidson likens this section of the Song to a curtain call which occurs at the end of a play or musical. He notes, 'One by one the lead characters come forward, take a bow, and through a characteristic action or by a few well-chosen words, recall what has gone before.'[1] In 8:6-7, the character who comes forward for a bow, and to speak a few well-chosen words, is the woman. Here the woman offers, through poetic imagery, the most articulate and extensive definition of true human love available in all of God's revelation. Although the entire Song deals with romantic human love, in these verses she is particularly focused on its essence. For example, the word 'love' is employed eleven times as a noun in the Song of Songs, three of which are in this couplet. In other words, the woman is trying to define true love for us, but she doesn't do it with the technical precision of science, instead she expresses its meaning through a series of metaphors and a proverb. By means of these literary devices the woman reveals that true love is exclusive, enduring and priceless. In the next three chapters we will look at each one of these elements. In this chapter we will delve into the rich beauty of this definition of true love by first looking at its exclusive nature.

Make me like a seal

As the woman unveils her definition of true love, she begins by using the metaphor of a 'seal'. She declares to her lover, 'Place me like a seal over your heart, like a seal on your arm.' In order to understand what this reveals about the nature of true love we must first understand how a seal functioned in the ancient world.

In the ancient Near East, seals were often used for the purpose of establishing identity, authenticity and possession. Often these ancient seals would contain some type of picture, word or design which linked the seal to its owner. The seal would be used to make an identifying and authenticating mark by impressing it on a material such as clay.[2] Most often these seals were worn around one's neck on a cord, thus hanging over the heart (Genesis 38:18); or they were worn as a signet ring on one's finger, thus becoming an extension of one's arm (Genesis

41:42; Jeremiah 22:24; and Haggai 2:23).[3] These seals were considered an extension of their owner and were equated with their owner's identity. In fact, they were so closely connected with their owner's identity that they were often buried with him at his death.[4] Therefore, they were invaluable and had to be protected at all costs. The importance of these items is evidenced by where they were worn. They were worn in safe locations such as near their owner's heart and on his finger. We see an example of how the seal served as an extension of its owner in an account recorded in Genesis.

Tamar and Judah

In Genesis 38, Tamar deceives Judah, her father-in-law, into sleeping with her by posing as a prostitute. Although our immediate reaction is to question her conduct, the Bible actually treats Tamar as a heroine because she is trying to preserve and continue the covenant line through Judah. However, before she is willing to give herself to him sexually, she wants to make sure she can prove that Judah is the father of any child she may conceive from this encounter. So how does Tamar guarantee that she can prove that Judah is the father of her child? The answer is found in their interchange in Genesis 38:18: 'He [Judah] said, "What pledge should I give you?" "*Your seal* and its cord, and the staff in your hand," she answered. So he gave them to her and slept with her, and she became pregnant by him,' (emphasis mine). Tamar demanded Judah's seal as a pledge because she understood that possessing his seal was the same as possessing Judah himself. It was the ultimate source of proof that Judah was the father of her child. In our day we worry about 'identity theft'. We worry about people coming into possession of our vital information and then posing as us. In the ancient Near East, your seal was your identity; it was an extension of yourself. When Tamar took possession of Judah's seal, she took possession of his identity.

The meaning of the seal

Now let us return to the woman's words in the Song of Songs. She declares to her lover that she wants him to treat her like his seal, to place her over his heart and on his arm. What she is really saying is that she desires her husband to possess her exclusively. She longs to give up her own identity, to become an extension of his. She desires to become part and parcel of him.

She yearns to surrender herself to him entirely, wholeheartedly and exclusively. Tremper Longman suggests that her desire to be marked on his heart and on his arm may indicate that she desired to be part of both his inner being (his 'heart') and his outward actions (his 'arm').[5] She wanted to be part of all he was and all he did. What we learn from her desire is that true love requires exclusivity. True love requires the giving of oneself exclusively to another so that one becomes an extension of that other person.

> True love requires the giving of oneself exclusively to another so that one becomes an extension of that other person.

67

It is important to point out that just because the woman is speaking here does not mean that this principle of exclusivity is solely for the woman. The Song of Songs makes it clear that the husband is to give his wife the same type of exclusive commitment. He is to treat her as his exclusive love. He is to forsake all others, including himself, in favour of her. We see an example of the principle of exclusivity being applied in the husband's context in chapter six of the Song where the man declares the following:

> Sixty queens there may be, and eighty concubines, and virgins beyond number; but my dove, my perfect one, is unique, the only daughter of her mother, the favourite of the one who bore her. The maidens saw her and called her blessed; the queens and concubines praised her
>
> (Song 6:8-9).

In these verses, the man is expressing his exclusive commitment to his true love by comparing her beauty to that of three classes of other women: queens, concubines and virgins. These are all potential suitors, but the man clearly states that his heart and affections are fixed only on his true love. She is superior to all. He demonstrates this by referring to her as his 'dove' and his 'perfect one' (6:9). He also declares that she is 'unique' (6:9). The man even goes so far as to compare his love to that of a mother for her favourite daughter. He states that his true love is 'the only daughter of her mother, the favourite of the one who bore her' (6:9). Finally, the superiority of his true love is affirmed by her potential competitors. The queens, concubines and virgins (or 'maidens') all voice their agreement on the uniqueness of his true love by praising her and calling her blessed (6:9). They all acknowledge that she has something which they do not — his love. In these verses the man declares that he has forsaken all others and given himself exclusively to her. True love requires both husband and wife to give themselves exclusively to each other.

The principle of exclusivity in the New Testament

The principle of exclusivity is not just an Old Testament idea, it is found in the New Testament as well. For example, in Matthew 19:4-5 Jesus explicitly teaches the principle of exclusivity by reiterating the teaching of Genesis: '"Haven't you read," he replied, "that at the beginning the Creator 'made them male and female', and said, *'For this reason a man will leave his father and mother and be united to his wife, and the two will become one flesh'?"'* (emphasis mine). Furthermore, the apostle Paul, in his Epistle to the Ephesians, declares that a wife is to give herself exclusively to her husband by submitting to him as to the Lord (Ephesians 5:22) and that the husband is in turn to give himself exclusively to his wife by imitating Christ's self-sacrifice for his bride, the church (5:24-27). In fact, Paul goes so far as to demand that the man is to love his wife as his own body (5:28-29). He is to love her as an extension of himself, of his own identity. The imagery expressed here is much like that of the seal of the ancient Near East. In effect, Paul commands the husband to place his wife like a seal over his heart, like a seal on his arm. Finally, in 1 Corinthians 7, the apostle reminds both husband and wife that their bodies are no longer their own, but are now owned exclusively by their spouse: 'The wife's body does not belong to her alone but also to her husband. In the same way, the husband's body does not belong to him alone but also to his wife,' (v. 4). In premarital counselling I often use this verse to impress upon the couple the exclusive demands of marriage. I charge them that once they are married their bodies become the exclusive property of their spouses. Marriage involves an exclusive giving of ourselves to our spouses.

While our culture may view marriage as a legal partnership in which both parties retain their own separate identities and autonomy, the Bible speaks of marriage as an exclusive relationship that inevitably leads to exchanging one's own separate identity and autonomy for a new mutually created identity. In biblical parlance, the two become *one* flesh: 'For this reason a man will leave his father and mother and be united to his wife, and they will become one flesh,' (Genesis 2:24), or as Jesus declared, 'So they are no longer two, but one. Therefore what God has joined together, let man not separate,' (Matthew 19:6). True love is exclusive.

Exercising exclusivity

There is an area off the south-eastern coast of the United States — encompassing the waters around Bermuda, Miami and San Juan — which is notorious for a series of unexplained ship and aircraft disappearances. There have been many attempts to explain why so many vessels have been lost in this area, ranging from environmental factors to the supernatural. While it may simply be coincidence, a myth, or superstition, what is undeniable is that it can be a dangerous thing to enter the troubled waters known as the 'Bermuda' or 'Devil's Triangle'.

The Bible also warns us about a dangerous triangle: a triangle which can threaten to shipwreck a marriage. The triangle I am referring to is created when a married couple allows a third party to intrude into their marriage relationship. Biblical scholar O. Palmer Robertson remarks as follows regarding the danger of triangulating the marriage relationship:

> The intimacies of the marriage relationship are of such a vitally personal nature that the intrusion of a third person into the scene invariably leads to the most intense manifestations of resentment to be found anywhere in human experience. Volumes have been written recounting the jealousies, the intrigues, the hatred, murder, and bad blood that has flowed as a consequence of a love-triangle.[6]

The reason triangulation is so devastating is because it is a violation of God's plan. God intended marriage to involve only two parties, one man and one woman. He emphasized the importance of this by commanding the man to 'leave his father and mother and be united to his wife' (Genesis 2:24). God told the man that he must first 'leave' one relationship (with his father and mother) in order to 'cleave' to his new relationship with his wife. In other words, from the very beginning God commanded husband and wife not to triangulate their relationship. God commanded the first couple, and by implication all couples, to exercise exclusivity.

Sources of triangulation

In order to maintain the exclusive nature of true love couples must be able to identify the potential sources of third-party intrusion. Of course, the most obvious, and most damaging, form of third-party intrusion occurs when one member of the couple becomes sexually intimate with another person of the opposite sex. We often refer to this situation as a 'love triangle'. The Bible contains many examples of the devastating impact of this type of triangulation. For instance, in O. Palmer Robertson's helpful book *The Genesis of Sex*, he provides two examples of the devastating consequences of this type of 'love triangle' both of which come from the book of Genesis.[7]

Abraham, Sarah and Hagar

The first example Robertson cites is that of Abraham, Sarah and Hagar. Frustrated by her inability to conceive, Sarah suggests to her husband that he attempt to conceive by having sexual relations with her young and fertile handmaid Hagar. Abraham agreed to this scheme and subsequently had sexual relations with Hagar. This encounter eventually yielded him a son, Ishmael. While this scheme clearly suggested unfaithfulness to the promises of God on the part of Abraham and Sarah, it also produced strife in their marriage relationship. Even though it was Sarah who originally suggested the liaison with Hagar, she eventually became so jealous of her that she declared the following to Abraham: 'You are responsible for the wrong I am suffering. I put my servant in your arms, and now that she knows she is pregnant, she despises me. May the LORD judge between you and me,' (Genesis 16:5). The end result of Abraham and Sarah's triangulation of their marriage was marital strife and discord.

Jacob, Rachel and Leah

The second example cited by Robertson is that of Jacob and his two wives, Rachel and Leah. This situation was doomed from the beginning. Jacob unwisely agreed to commence his married life in a triangulated relationship. His marriage began with his wives pitted as fierce rivals for his affection and what made matters worse was that Rachel and Leah, as sisters, already shared a sibling rivalry prior to becoming rivals as wives. As Robertson notes, the main source of their rivalry as wives was in the area of providing children for Jacob. These two women became engaged in a competition for their husband's affections and each one was hoping to win by giving him heirs. Leah got off to a head start by giving birth to six sons before Rachel gave birth to her first. However, Rachel's son Joseph was special and he quickly became Jacob's favourite. Rachel had emerged victorious in the competition and she announced her victory in no uncertain terms: 'I have had a great struggle with my sister, and I have won,' (Genesis 30:8). This rivalry between Rachel and Leah not only created strife in Jacob's marriage, but it also had severe ramifications for the next generation of his family. Because Rachel's son Joseph was Jacob's favourite, this led to great jealousy among Jacob's other sons, particularly among those mothered by Leah. This jealousy eventually led Joseph's brothers to sell him into slavery. Once again, marital triangulation yielded disharmony and division.

These two biblical examples clearly demonstrate the devastating consequences which result from bringing a third party into the marriage relationship in the form of a 'love triangle'. O. Palmer Robertson enumerates these consequences:

> The love triangle can only bring unhappiness, heartache, strife, contention, jealousy, hatred, murder, and devastated lives. From the beginning it has been God's intent to have only two people joined in the intimacies of love. His fullest blessing will rest only on those who live according to his design.[8]

God's design is for one man and one woman to come together in an exclusive sexual relationship.

Other sources of triangulation

Pornography and the 'emotional love triangle'

The two examples we have looked at so far both involved a 'love triangle' which was created when one member of the couple engaged in a direct sexual relationship with a third party. However, there are other ways in which a marriage can become triangulated.

For example, the viewing of pornography by one member of the couple creates the functional equivalent of a love triangle. When a married person views pornography he or she is bringing a third person into their marriage. Just think about it for a moment. How would your spouse feel if she caught you gazing through binoculars at your neighbour while he or she was undressing? Do you consider this any different from gazing at an undressed person through a computer? Pornography destroys exclusivity because it makes another person a rival to your spouse. We are living in an age of virtual adultery. Therefore, instead of indulging the lust of the eyes (1 John 2:16), make a covenant with your eyes to avoid the deadly trap of

> God's design is for one man and one woman to come together in an exclusive sexual relationship.

pornography. Follow the example of Job, 'I made a covenant with my eyes not to look lustfully at a girl,' (Job 31:1).

Triangulation can also occur when one member of the couple gives themselves emotionally to a third party, when they develop an emotionally intimate relationship with someone other than their spouse. This creates an emotional love triangle which can be just as devastating as a sexual love triangle. This form of triangulation frequently arises in the workplace. It is often the case that spouses spend more time each day with their business associates than with one another. It is very tempting to develop close emotional relationships with these associates, particularly those of the opposite sex. Often these relationships begin to include the sharing of intimacies which should be reserved solely for the marital relationship. This type of emotional sharing is wrong even if it never leads to physical intimacy. There is such a thing as emotional adultery. Christians must avoid triangulating their marriages through emotional love triangles.

Work, friends, family and recreation

While our work, friends, families and recreation are all wonderful blessings, they can also become destructive if they are allowed to intrude too far into the heart of the marriage relationship or if they develop into rivals to our spouses. It is very easy for us to allow these otherwise good things to so consume our affections and time that we neglect our spouses because of them. For example, pursuing career ambitions can lead one to be away from their spouse so much that there is no time to cultivate a romantic loving relationship. When I practised law I often heard the saying, 'The law is a jealous mistress.' The point of this saying is that the legal profession can quickly become the 'other woman' in a marriage. It can begin to demand more and more of you so that you neglect your wife. I felt these pressures when I practised law. However, this proverb is not only applicable to the legal profession; it applies across the board to all types of careers. In fact, there is a particular risk in this area for those men and women who serve in full-time Christian ministry. It is very easy for those engaged in callings of this order to excuse the neglect of their spouses with platitudes about serving God. How many pastors' wives are unduly neglected for the sake of the congregation? If you are married, regardless of your calling, you have an obligation not to make your calling a rival to your spouse.

In addition to the temptations of career, it is possible for a marriage to be triangulated by family or friends. This type of triangulation occurs when a member of a family or a close friend begins to exert so much influence in a marriage that they actually undermine marital communication and trust. This most often occurs when one spouse is so inordinately dependent on their parents that they allow their parents to intrude into the heart of their marital relationship. If you first turn to a friend or family member for advice instead of your spouse then you are at risk of triangulating your marriage.

Finally, recreation can also become a potential source of triangulation in a marriage. When this particular source of triangulation emerges it is normally the fault of the husband. It is often the case that men are more interested in collecting and using their 'toys' than they are in spending time with their wives. When a husband places his leisure time above the needs of his wife he is making his recreation a rival to his wife. A Christian husband must not allow this triangulation to occur in his marriage.

Children as a potential source of triangulation

There is an even more subtle third-party threat to the marriage relationship. It is possible for a couple's own children to emerge as an intrusive rival to their own romantic relationship. Everyone who has had a child knows that children are extremely needy and demanding. My wife and I recently learned the truth of this after we adopted our first child. We quickly realized that it was quite easy to neglect one another in the face of the immense responsibility of caring for an infant, particularly when we were both suffering from sleep deprivation! However, it is not just infant children who pose a threat to the marriage relationship.

In our age many parents fall into the trap of organizing their home around the needs of older children who are engaged in a vast array of activities. These couples spend their time as chauffeurs for their children while their own relationship suffers. Couples who make children the centre of their marriage often experience devastating and lasting consequences to their marriages — consequences which only become apparent after the children are gone. For example, Christian counsellor Jay Adams notes that couples who make their children the focal point of their marriages often find no marriage relationship left after their children leave home.[9] Couples who make the parent-child relationship primary often fail to cultivate the husband-wife relationship. By making children the focal point of the home, couples run the risk of unwittingly allowing themselves to grow apart. Just consider how many divorces occur in our society after the children have left home.

Clearly, raising children is an important activity in God's kingdom. However, when couples allow child rearing to become so all-consuming that they neglect their own romantic relationship it not only harms their relationship, but it ultimately harms their children as well. For example, Jay Adams notes that when couples make the parent-child relationship primary they actually end up depriving their children.[10] Adams suggests that this deprivation occurs because parents who make their children the centre of their lives fail to set a good example of a healthy husband and wife relationship for their children. Children raised under such circumstances are more likely to grow up and repeat the same error in their marriages. In addition, Adams notes that parents who make children the centre of their lives often have difficulty letting go of their children when they get married. Because they made their children the centre of their lives they are tempted to keep them there. This temptation often produces strife in the marriages of their children.[11] Therefore, couples who let their children become the centre of their marriage are not only damaging their own marriage, but they are also sowing the seeds which may well damage the marriages of their children as well.

How to avoid triangulation

So how can couples protect themselves against third-party intrusions? How can couples prevent triangulation in their marriages? This is an admittedly difficult task and it requires constant vigilance. However, the following are a few steps which couples can take to reduce the threat of triangulation.

First, couples must commit to continually work together to establish and maintain mutually agreed upon boundaries to these other relationships of life. This means that couples must frequently assess whether work, friends, family, recreation, or even their children, are intruding inappropriately into their marriage relationship.

Second, couples must make certain that they are scheduling time to be alone as a couple. It is vital for couples to carve out time just for themselves. In fact, one of the ways that couples can determine if they are keeping their marriage as the primary relationship is by examining their calendar to see what is dominating their life. It is very easy in this busy age for couples to fill their calendars with a variety of activities and neglect being together as husband and wife. For example, my wife and I are involved in a busy pastorate in a college community with many activities. Our schedule is so busy that we find it necessary

> It is very easy in this busy age for couples to fill their calendars with a variety of activities and neglect being together as husband and wife.

to keep a three-month calendar on our refrigerator just to keep things straight. One of the things we do to protect our exclusive time is to set aside time on our calendar just for us. We simply mark off days for us as husband and wife and we treat these days as an inviolable commitment to one another. There is nothing inappropriate about telling someone you cannot attend a function because you want, and need, to be with your spouse. Christian couples must set aside time to be together exclusively.

Third, if you are a couple with children, analyse the time you are spending on your children and their extra-curricular activities. Perhaps a child does not need to engage in three sports, maybe one will suffice. Perhaps they do not need to ride horses *and* play a musical instrument *and* participate in the school play *and* take karate lessons. If the scale has tipped so far that your children are the centre of your home it is time for a rebalancing.

Finally, couples must always remember that after their relationship with God, the marriage relationship is the *primary* relationship of their life. They must never forget that they are always husband and wife before they are employers or employees, sons or daughters, fathers or mothers. When couples fail to keep first things first, when they fail to exercise exclusivity in their marriages, this failure not only impacts the marriage relationship, but it also impacts all the other relationships and duties of life. For example, couples who fail to exercise exclusivity in their marriages often find that they are less able to honour their own parents, raise their children, help in their churches, serve in their communities, maintain effective friendships and glorify God in the workplace. By keeping your marriage relationship primary you will find that you are better able to serve Christ effectively in every sphere of life.

I began this section by using the Bermuda Triangle as an illustration; let me close this section by referring once again to this mysterious place. The Bermuda Triangle is one of two places on earth where a magnetic compass points to true north, rather than magnetic north. This is known as a 'compass variation'. If a navigator of a vessel does not adjust for this variation he will eventually find himself way off course. Even though the variation is only slight at first, the longer he fails to adjust for it, the further he will drift off course. A similar dynamic can occur in a marriage in which the couple does not exercise the exclusivity of true love. At first it may seem that their failure to protect their marriage from third-party intrusions will only impact their marriage slightly, but as time goes by the couple may find themselves further and further off course. They may find themselves adrift in troubled waters, lost at sea. In order to avoid such a fate couples must continually ensure they exercise the exclusive nature of their love.

The most exclusive love of all

One of the ways to encourage yourself to exercise exclusivity in your marriage is by considering the exclusive nature of

God's love for his bride. The Bible teaches us that God's love for his people is an exclusive love. God treats his church as his exclusive 'treasured possession': 'For you are a people holy to the LORD your God. The LORD your God has chosen you out of all the peoples on the face of the earth to be his people, his treasured possession,' (Deuteronomy 7:6).[12] The principle of exclusivity is at the heart of the main covenant promise of the Bible: 'And I heard a loud voice from the throne saying, "Now the dwelling of God is with men, and he will live with them. *They will be his people, and God himself will be with them and be their God"'* (Revelation 21:3, emphasis mine). The Old Testament book of Hosea reminds us that while the people of God may stray from their faithfulness, God's love and loyalty remains exclusively fixed on them and them alone. God's love entertains no rivals. His love for us is exclusive. Therefore, imitate God by loving your spouse in a similar manner.

Questions for review and discussion

1. *Ask yourself the following question, 'Am I violating the command to give myself exclusively to my spouse?' Examine yourself to see if you are allowing a third party into your marriage in the form of a person of the opposite sex at work, a pornographic image on a computer, an old college friend, a form of recreation, your career, or even your parents. Make a list of things which you think are intruding into your relationship with your spouse. After compiling the list, discuss it with your spouse to see if he or she concurs with your analysis. After discussing the matter, pray together and specifically ask God to*

help you set appropriate boundaries and to practise the principle of marital exclusivity.

2. Read Proverbs 5:15-20 and contemplate and discuss how this passage calls you to sexual exclusivity with your spouse.

3. Read Exodus 20:1-7; Deuteronomy 6:4-9; and Matthew 22:37-40. What do these passages reveal about the type of love we owe to God?

4. Read Exodus 34:12-15; Leviticus 20:5-6; Judges 2:17; Isaiah 6:9; Jeremiah 3:1-9; Ezekiel 16:30-32; and Revelation 17:1-5. Note how these passages connect spiritual adultery to spiritual apostasy. Contemplate and discuss how these passages apply to your relationship with God and to your relationship with your spouse.

5. The nature of true love: enduring

Believe me, if all those endearing young charms

Believe me, if all those endearing young charms,
Which I gaze on so fondly today,
Were to change by tomorrow, and fleet in my arms,
Like fairy-gifts fading away,
Thou wouldst still be adored, as this moment thou art,
Let thy loveliness fade as it will,
And around the dear ruin each wish of my heart
Would entwine itself verdantly still.

It is not while beauty and youth are thine own,
And thy cheeks unprofaned by a tear
That the fervour and faith of a soul can be known,
To which time will but make thee more dear;
No, the heart that has truly loved never forgets,
But as truly loves on to the close,
As the sunflower turns on her god, when he sets,
The same look which she turned when he rose.

(Thomas Moore)

What the Bible teaches about marriage

'Place me like a seal over your heart, like a seal on your arm;
for love is as strong as death, its jealousy unyielding as the grave.
It burns like blazing fire, like a mighty flame.
Many waters cannot quench love; rivers cannot wash it away.
If one were to give all the wealth of his house for love,
it would be utterly scorned'
(Song of Songs 8:6-7).

In the previous chapter we saw how the woman utilizes the metaphor of the seal to reveal the exclusive nature of true love. However, the seal is not the only metaphor she uses to teach us about the nature of true love. In the second part of verse six and the first part of verse seven she uses two additional metaphors, death and fire, to explain a second attribute of true love. Through the imagery of these metaphors she declares that true love is irreversible, insatiable and inextinguishable. In other words, the woman declares that true love is an enduring love.

True love endures because it is irreversible

One of my favourite films is *The Princess Bride*. In that movie, the main character, Wesley, is passionately in love with a woman named Buttercup. He endures numerous trials as he attempts to be reunited with Buttercup after a long separation. At one point, Wesley even experiences death momentarily. After he is revived and encounters Buttercup he passionately declares to her that, 'Death cannot stop true love. All it can do is delay it for a while.' Of course, Wesley's point is that true love is stronger than death. That is similar to, although not quite the same as, the meaning of the words we find in verse six where the woman describes true love as being 'as strong as death' (8:6). Her point is not that true love conquers death, but rather that true love is like death in that it is irreversible.

The Bible often portrays death as a ferocious enemy which seeks to irreversibly conquer us, overtake us and possess us. Tom Gledhill describes the Old Testament view of death as follows: '*Death* is an active power, holding its victims in its irresistible sway and none can escape. *Death* claims those under its power, and draws them into its grip.'[1] An example of this view of death may be witnessed in the following verses from Psalm 18: 'The cords of death entangled me; the torrents of destruction overwhelmed me. The cords of the grave coiled around me; the snares of death confronted me,' (Psalm 18:4-5). In these verses David depicts death as a force which is trying to claim and bind him for ever. The woman in the Song of Songs is saying that true love has similar attributes. Once it wraps its cords around the object of its affection, true love never lets go. It holds its prey for ever. The woman is saying that true love is *like* death in its ferocity and irreversibility. I think Tom Gledhill accurately captures the thrust of her point in his commentary on the Song of Songs:

> It is not the case here that love survives death, that love is stronger than death, but rather that love holds its victims under its sway in exactly the same way as death does. Once smitten there is no escape. The process is one-way and irreversible. Love binds those under its sway with a permanent bond.[2]

87

What the woman is saying is that true love endures because it is as irreversible as death itself.

True love endures because it is insatiable

In her definition of true love the woman not only uses the metaphor of death to reveal the enduring *irreversibility* of true love, but she also uses it to demonstrate the enduring *insatiableness* of true love. In the final section of Song 8:6, the woman proclaims that her love is as 'unyielding as the grave'. The word 'grave' is, of course, a synonym for death. In the Old Testament, the 'grave' is frequently likened to a creature with an open mouth, or throat, which seeks to devour human life. The Old Testament also indicates that the appetite of the grave is insatiable. For example, consider the following texts:

- *Proverbs 30:15-16*: 'The leech has two daughters. "Give! Give!" they cry. There are three things that are never satisfied, four that never say, "Enough!": *the grave*, the barren womb, land, which is *never satisfied* with water, and fire, which never says, "Enough!"' (emphasis mine).
- *Habakkuk 2:5*: '[I]ndeed, wine betrays him; he is arrogant and never at rest. Because he is *as greedy as the grave* and *like death is never satisfied*, he gathers to himself all the nations and takes captive all the peoples,' (emphasis mine).
- *Isaiah 5:14*: 'Therefore *the grave enlarges its appetite* and *opens its mouth without limit*; into it will descend their nobles and masses with all their brawlers and revellers,' (emphasis mine).

According to the Bible, the grave has an appetite which is gluttonous, voracious and insatiable. It possesses a hunger which never abates. The woman describes true love in similar terms. She states that, like the grave, true love has an unyielding hunger. As Ian Provan notes in his commentary on the Song, '...the passion that lovers share is as stubborn and unrelenting as the underworld, which pursues all living things to swallow them up'.[3] True love endures because it possesses an appetite which is as insatiable as the grave. However, the metaphor of the grave is not the only way by which the woman brings out the insatiable nature of true love in this text.

The second way she expresses the insatiable nature of true love is by equating true love with jealousy. She does this by means of synonymous parallelism. In verse six she matches 'love' with 'jealousy' and 'death' with 'grave'. Note the parallelism of verse six as it is depicted in the following diagram:

for **love** is as strong as ... **death,**
↓ ↓
its **jealousy** unyielding as the **grave**

The woman declares that true love contains a jealousy which is insatiable, it is as 'unyielding as the grave'.

Now at first the suggestion that love and jealousy are in some way synonymous may seem very peculiar to a modern reader. In our culture today we have been programmed to think of jealousy as a solely negative emotion, one which we should avoid. It is true that the Bible tells us that jealousy is often the root of destructive sinful patterns of behaviour. For instance, consider the example of King Saul. In 1 Samuel we learn that Saul was a man besieged with jealousy regarding David: 'And from that time on Saul kept a *jealous* eye on David,' (1 Samuel 18:9, emphasis mine). Saul became insanely jealous of David and this led him to engage in all types of sins, including the attempted murder of David. There is no doubt that the Bible warns us to avoid sinful expressions of jealousy.

It is important to note, however, that the Bible does not teach that jealousy is *always* sinful. For instance, God describes himself as a 'jealous God' in the Second Commandment:

> You shall not make for yourself an idol in the form of anything in heaven above or on the earth beneath or in the waters below. You shall not bow down to them or worship them; for I, the LORD your God, *am a jealous God*, punishing the children for the sin of the fathers to the third and fourth generation of those who hate me,
> (Exodus 20:4-5, emphasis mine).

There are other texts which reveal that jealousy is an attribute of God. For example, consider the following:

- *Deuteronomy 4:24*: 'For the LORD your God is a consuming fire, *a jealous God*,' (emphasis mine).
- *Nahum 1:2*: '*The LORD is a jealous* and avenging God; the LORD takes vengeance and is filled with wrath. The LORD takes vengeance on his foes and maintains his wrath against his enemies,' (emphasis mine).
- *Zechariah 1:14*: 'Then the angel who was speaking to me said, "Proclaim this word: This is what the LORD Almighty

says: *'I am very jealous for Jerusalem* and Zion,'"' (emphasis mine).

The Bible reveals that God is a jealous God. He is jealous for his people to worship, love and serve him alone. He is jealous for the affections of his bride and will not tolerate any form of spiritual adultery. He demands an enduring commitment from his bride. Clearly, given that jealousy is an attribute of God, it cannot be inherently sinful. However, does this mean that humans are also capable of exercising a godly form of jealousy? The New Testament reveals that we can.

The apostle Paul speaks of jealousy as a positive emotion, one he himself both possesses and exercises. For example, in 2 Corinthians 11:2 Paul speaks of his jealousy for the people in the church at Corinth: 'I am jealous for you with a godly jealousy. I promised you to one husband, to Christ, so that I might present you as a pure virgin to him.' What is fascinating about this verse, particularly given our consideration of the use of the word 'jealousy' in the Song of Songs, is that Paul employs jealousy in a positive sense in the context of a marriage relationship — our heavenly marriage to Christ. Paul's jealousy is driven by his desire to see his people betrothed to Christ. It is as if Paul views his role as bringing the church to Christ, to give her away to her husband, and

> God is a jealous God. He is jealous for his people to worship, love and serve him alone ... He demands an enduring commitment from his bride.

he is jealous to see this marriage consummated. The great Princeton theologian Charles Hodge notes the power of this wedding imagery in his commentary on 2 Corinthians 11:2 in which he writes of Paul:

> He may compare himself in this verse to a father who gives his daughter to the bridegroom... Paul's relation was so intimate with the Corinthians as the author of their espousals to Christ, that he could not fail to feel the deepest interest in their fidelity... Paul's desire was that the Corinthians should remain faithful to their vows...[4]

In other words, Paul was jealous to see the Corinthians remain faithful to their bridegroom. He would endure any cost to see them united.

What can we conclude from this? I think we can conclude that jealousy is an appropriate emotion in the context of divine-human love and in the context of the human love shared between a husband and a wife. This makes sense when we remember that the love shared between a husband and wife is analogous to God's love for his people. When God made humanity in his image, both male and female, he called them to imitate him. God's love for his spouse is a jealous love and, therefore, human spouses are to love one another with a similar jealousy. But how does jealousy relate to the theme of insatiability?

Jealousy connects to the theme of insatiability because jealousy, like the appetite of the grave, is gluttonous. Commentator Tom Gledhill aptly captures the insatiable nature of godly jealousy when he writes:

Such is the *jealousy* of *love*. It is the emotion of single-minded devotion, which when turned away from self, produces overpowering zeal to promote the undivided glory of the person who is loved. The negative connotations of jealousy must surely be absent here. So perhaps it may best be translated by 'single-minded passion'. There is virtually no hint in the Song of the self-destructive envy that arises from frustrated love due to intrusion of a rival party. The morbid gratification of endless introspection, the intolerance of another's happiness or good fortune, the ceaseless self-destructive desire to inflict pain on one whose happiness is denied to oneself — this too is as unyielding as Sheol. But the Song is singing of the all-embracing jealousy of love, its zeal, its passion, its ardour which will brook no rivals.[5]

This is how the concept of jealousy connects with the theme of insatiability. Jealousy is an emotion which is never satisfied. It is single-minded and unswerving in its pursuit. Its zeal never gives way. The Song tells us that the love shared between a husband and a wife is to be marked by a single-minded, all-encompassing jealousy. Spousal love must possess a jealousy which is unyielding as the grave.

The woman declares that true love is enduring because it possesses an insatiable appetite like the grave and an insatiable jealousy which mimics the jealous love of God for his people. The hunger of true love never ends. True love endures because it is insatiable.

True love endures because it is inextinguishable

As the woman continues to build on her description of the enduring nature of true love she employs yet another metaphor. She declares that true love is like fire. At the end of verse six and the beginning of verse seven she states that love 'burns like blazing fire, like a mighty flame. Many waters cannot quench love; rivers cannot wash it away,' (8:6-7). In these verses she compares love to a violent fire burning with intense heat. The phrase 'like a mighty flame' is meant to express the superlative nature of this flame.[6] The point she is making is that true love is not just some small controlled burn, but rather it is a wildfire. And the fire of true love is so indefatigable, so enduring, that it cannot be extinguished even by fire's greatest enemy — water. In verse seven the woman boldly proclaims that, 'Many waters cannot quench love; rivers cannot wash it away,' (8:7). In order to grasp the full meaning of her words we must first understand the significance of water in the ancient Hebrew psyche.

In our modern world, most of us do not fear the power of water. For most of us, water is something that flows gently out of a tap. However, one of the greatest fears of the ancient Hebrew was that of water, particularly the fear of overwhelming waters like those unleashed by God during the time of Noah. This fear manifests itself frequently in the Psalms. The psalmist often describes his turmoil and trouble through the metaphor of 'many' or 'mighty' waters (Psalm 18:4-5,16; 32:6; & 144:7). In fact, the Old Testament reveals that these 'many' or 'mighty' waters are so powerful that only God can control them (Psalm 29:3; 77:19; & 93:4). Although most of us cannot grasp this ancient Hebrew fear of water, we have been reminded of the devastating effects of water by the recent tsunami disaster in Indonesia and the destruction wrought by Hurricane Katrina in the Gulf Coast of the United States. The survivors of these disasters can relate quite well to the fear of 'many' or 'mighty' waters. Water remains a powerful and, at times, overwhelming force.

Therefore, what the woman is saying in the Song is that these overwhelming waters, which struck fear into the hearts of the Hebrews and which were so powerful that they could only be controlled by God himself, are insufficient to snuff out the fervent flame of true love. She is declaring that true love is not a 'flash in the pan'. According to the Song of Songs, true love is not a burst of flame which momentarily erupts like a volcano only to quickly fade into dormancy. Rather, the Song teaches us that true love possesses a flame which does not fade with time and which cannot be extinguished even by its most formidable foe. True love not only burns hot, but it also burns long. The flames of true love do not blow out in the face of winds of adversity nor are they quenched by the waters of turmoil. The woman uses the metaphor of fire to demonstrate that true love endures, even in the face of opposition. As one commentator put it, 'The tenacious staying power of love is set against these tides and perennial rivers which are unable either to wash love away or put out its sparks.'[7] True love endures like an inextinguishable flame.

Fan the flame of true love

As we have seen in this chapter, one of the marks of true love is that it endures. True love is not fickle, but rather it is steadfast in its commitment. However, true love can only endure if it is cultivated and nurtured. The metaphor of the flame used by the woman in the Song is a helpful way to think about this need to nurture romantic love. In order for a flame to continue to burn it must be cared for and fed. Couples must do a similar thing with their love. If a couple desire their love to endure they must tend it like a flame, they must fan the flame of true love.

After American President John F. Kennedy was assassinated he was buried in Arlington National Cemetery in Virginia. To honour the legacy of the fallen president, his wife suggested that his grave be marked with an eternal flame. Mrs Kennedy lit this flame at his funeral in 1963 and it has been burning ever since. The burner used at President Kennedy's gravesite was specially engineered to avoid being extinguished by wind or rain. The burner, which was developed by the Institute of Gas Technology of Chicago, includes a constantly recurring electric spark which guarantees that the flame will not go out. The flames of marital love must be maintained in a similar way; they must be repeatedly sparked.

However, there are many things which distract us from fanning the flame of true love. It is easy for couples to forget the need to be vigilant in this respect as they live out their busy lives together. For example, in his book *The Life of a God-Made Man* Dan Doriani notes the danger of allowing the flame of love to be extinguished by being consumed by the many daily duties we have as spouses. Doriani notes that there are two main components to the marital relationship.[8] He describes these two components to the relationship as 'positional orientations'.

First, there is the 'side-by-side' component of the marriage relationship. What Doriani means by this is that married couples are to face and engage the world together. They are to jointly serve Christ, shoulder to shoulder, in all realms of life. Couples do this every day as they manage the house, go to work and raise children. However, there is a second positional orientation which couples must practise.

The second component of the marriage relationship is what Doriani refers to as the 'face-to-face' component. This is the romantic and passionate aspect of marriage. Couples experience this component of marriage when they gaze longingly into each other's eyes, share a romantic meal and enjoy physical intimacy.

A strong and healthy marriage will include both of these two components in equal measure. However, as Doriani points out, it is all too easy for couples to allow the 'face-to-face' component of their marriage to fizzle as the 'side-by-side' component becomes ever more demanding. Doriani comments on this danger:

> As the years roll by, as children and career and worthy causes press upon us, even a good marriage can devolve into little more than a co-labouring with a nice person of the opposite sex who shares our bed and kitchen. The relationship becomes ever more side-by-side, and the face-to-face recedes.[9]

Given this tendency for the 'face-to-face' to recede, married couples must be ever diligent in fanning the flame of true love. Much like a campfire or a fire in a fireplace, it must be

> **The flame of our love is not meant to go out in a blaze of glory, but ... to burn at an enduring and sustained pace.**

stoked and fed if it is to continue to burn strongly. As we have seen in this chapter, true love has an insatiable appetite. It must be fed continually. It is endlessly jealous for affection. Remember, the flame of our love is not meant to go out in a blaze of glory, but rather to burn at an enduring and sustained pace. So how can couples fan the flame of love? Let me provide you with a few suggestions:

1. *Remember to continue to court.* You can continue to fan the flame of love by remembering to woo your spouse. Set aside time for romantic encounters. Let your spouse know that you long to be with him or her, as do the lovers in the Song. They frequently express a desire to be alone together. For example, the Song closes with the woman reflecting this desire by declaring to her husband, 'Come away, my lover...' (Song of Songs 8:14). Make sure you continue to call your lover to 'come away'. Courtship should not end after you say 'I do.'

2. *Remember the power of a romantic, purposeful and gentle touch.* Hold your lover's hand, caress your lover's cheek, put your arm around your lover and firmly embrace your lover. We see the lovers in the Song longing for, and engaging in, this type of romantic touch. For example, in Song of Songs 2:6 the woman dreams of experiencing her lover's embrace, 'His left arm is under my head, and his right arm embraces

me.' Purposeful and romantic touch can communicate volumes. Touch is an integral part of fanning the flame. Do not underestimate its power.

3. *Remember to gaze longingly into your lover's eyes.* Much can be communicated through a simple glance in which your eyes meet those of your spouse. The man in the Song had his love enflamed by just 'one glance' from his lover's eyes (Song of Songs 4:9). Let your lover see the gleam in your eye.

4. *Remember to continue giving your lover special gifts and tokens of your affection.* The lovers in the Song often relate their love to perfumes, spices, jewellery, flowers and sweet-tasting foods. These tokens speak powerfully to the joy and ecstasy of love. Even in our modern culture we continue to consider gifts of perfume, flowers and chocolate as tokens of love. Remember to continue sharing these emblems of ecstasy with your spouse. Give your spouse fine gifts (i.e. perfume, flowers, jewellery, etc.) or simple, yet thoughtful, gifts (i.e. a romantic note under your spouse's pillow).

5. *Remember the power of poetry.* There is amazing power in romantic language. We see this in the Song of Songs. It is no coincidence that God chose the vehicle of poetry to reveal the beauty, joy and bliss of true love. Poetry has a particular power to capture the essence of romantic love. Therefore, be poetic with your spouse. Read the Song of Songs with your spouse or read your spouse a poem like 'How do I love thee?' by Elizabeth Barrett Browning:

How do I love thee? Let me count the ways.
I love thee to the depth and breadth and height
My soul can reach, when feeling out of sight
For the ends of Being and ideal Grace.
I love thee to the level of every day's
Most quiet need, by sun and candlelight.
I love thee freely, as men strive for right;
I love thee purely, as they turn from praise.
I love with a passion put to use
In my old griefs, and with my childhood's faith.
I love thee with a love I seemed to lose
With my lost saints — I love thee with the breath,
Smiles, tears, of all my life! — and, if God choose,
I shall but love thee better after death.

In order to keep the flame of love burning a couple must be jointly committed to feeding it. Like the eternal flame which marks the grave of President Kennedy, your relationship must have a constant sparking mechanism which keeps the flame of your love from going out.

The most enduring love of all

There are many things couples can do which can inspire them to cultivate an enduring love in their marriage, but perhaps the most powerful is simply considering the nature of God's enduring love for his people. God's love for his people burns like an eternal flame, even when his people are unfaithful. Many commentators have noticed an interesting parallel

100

between the definition of human love in Song of Songs 8:6-7 and the definition of God's love found in Isaiah 43:2. Note the similarity of themes in these two texts:

Song of Songs 8:6-7: '...for love is as strong as death, its jealousy unyielding as the grave. It burns like blazing fire, like a mighty flame. Many waters cannot quench love; rivers cannot wash it away...'

Isaiah 43:2: 'When you pass through the waters, I will be with you; and when you pass through the rivers, they will not sweep over you. When you walk through the fire, you will not be burned; the flames will not set you ablaze.'

Both texts use the imagery of the two most powerful natural forces known to mankind: fire and water. In Isaiah 43:2 God comforted his exiled people by telling them that they would not be overwhelmed by water or scorched by fire because of his enduring commitment to them. God never forsakes the people he loves. He makes a similar promise to the new covenant church in Hebrews 13:5 where he declares, 'Never will I leave you; never will I forsake you.' Jesus echoes this enduring commitment of love in the Great Commission when he promises the following, 'And surely I am with you always, to the very end of the age,' (Matthew 28:20). God's love for his people is an enduring love. The psalmist particularly extols God for his enduring love in Psalm 118:1: 'Give thanks to the LORD, for he is good; his love endures for ever.' Imitate God in your marriage by sharing an enduring love with your spouse.

Questions for review and discussion

1. *Read Numbers 23:19; Lamentations 3:21-23; and James 1:17. How do these texts reveal the irreversible nature of God's love and promises for his people? How should the promises of these texts be emulated in your marriage?*
2. *Read Malachi 2:14-16. How does this text speak to the enduring nature of true love? What does it require of spouses?*
3. *Contemplate and discuss the topic of jealousy as it relates to both divine and human love. Attempt to differentiate between godly and sinful forms of jealousy in the marriage relationship. Ask yourself whether you have a single-minded jealous human love for your spouse. Also ask yourself whether you are rendering devoted love to God. Are you keeping the Second Commandment (Exodus 20:4-5)?*
4. *Discuss with your spouse what steps you can take as a couple to maintain a constantly recurring spark in your marriage relationship. Make a list of suggested courses of action. Make a commitment to employ one of these suggestions next week.*
5. *The Bible reveals that God cultivates his love with his bride in a variety of ways. For instance, he spends time with her in communion and nurtures her with his Word and his sacraments. God is attentive to his bride and her needs. Like a loving husband, he woos his bride and adorns her. Read the following texts and note how God expresses his love to his spouse: Ezekiel 16:6-14; Isaiah 61:10; Ephesians 5:25-27; and Revelation 21:2. Contemplate and discuss how couples can emulate these practices in the marriage context.*

6. The nature of true love: priceless

The clod and the pebble

Love seeketh not itself to please,
Nor for itself hath any care,
But for another gives its ease
And builds a Heaven in Hell's despair.

(William Blake)

♦ ♦ ♦ ♦

'Place me like a seal over your heart, like a seal on your arm;
for love is as strong as death, its jealousy unyielding as the grave.
It burns like blazing fire, like a mighty flame.
Many waters cannot quench love; rivers cannot wash it away.
If one were to give all the wealth of his house for love,
it would be utterly scorned'
(Song of Songs 8:6-7).

While I was in the process of writing this book, the credit card company 'MasterCard' was featuring a series of commercials which attempted to display how their credit card helps a person to enjoy life more fully. The commercials begin with a person purchasing some consumer items which eventually allows them to engage in an intangible experience which is 'priceless'. The commercials conclude with the narrator making the following statement: 'There are some things money can't buy. For everything else, there's MasterCard.' These commercials are so subtly clever. At one level they attempt to communicate the principle that there are intangible experiences which cannot be purchased, experiences which are 'priceless', but at the same time these commercials insinuate that these experiences are more likely to be attained by buying things, particularly with the help of their credit card! Ultimately, the commercials subtly assert the very thing which they overtly deny. They suggest that you can buy your way to intangible and 'priceless' experiences. While MasterCard attempts to connect intangible experiences to commercial transactions, the woman in the Song of Songs utterly rejects such attempts.

In the previous two chapters we have seen how she describes the first two attributes of true love through a variety of metaphors including a seal, death and fire. However, as she unfolds the third attribute of true love, its priceless nature, she does not immediately turn to metaphor, but rather she begins by employing the following proverbial statement: 'If one were to give all the wealth of his house for love, it would be utterly scorned,' (Song of Songs 8:7). By means of this proverb the woman teaches us that true love is priceless. The woman spurns all efforts to treat love like a commodity which can be bought and sold. In fact, she states that even the attempt to put a price on it should be met with scorn. In other words, unlike MasterCard, the woman declares that acquiring true love is in no way related to a commercial transaction.

From proverb to parable

Although the woman initially uses a proverb-like statement to make her point, she quickly resumes her usual pattern of using metaphor. For example, just a few verses after issuing this proverb the woman again addresses the issue of the priceless nature of true love, but this time she conveys this message through a parable which uses as its centrepiece the metaphor of a vineyard. In Song 8:11 we learn that Solomon possessed a vineyard which he leased to tenants for a handsome sum: 'Solomon had a vineyard in Baal Hamon; he let out his vineyard to tenants. Each was to bring for its fruit a thousand shekels of silver.' However, in the very next verse the woman notes that she also possesses a vineyard, but instead of putting a price on it, like Solomon, she makes the following contrast: 'But my own vineyard is mine to give; the thousand shekels are for you, O Solomon, and two hundred are for those who tend its fruit,' (Song 8:12).[1] What is the point of this parable?

The point of the parable is that love cannot be bought. What she is saying is that even a rich and powerful man like King Solomon cannot buy her love. The woman teaches this lesson by making the 'vineyard' in this parable a metaphor for her love. Solomon may be able to own, buy, sell and rent his real estate (his vineyard), but he cannot do the same with her love (her vineyard).[2] She states this unequivocally in verse 12 by declaring that her vineyard, her love, is not a thing for sale. Instead, her love is hers 'to give' to whomever she chooses. By means of this parable the woman teaches the exact same principle she first unfolded in Song 8:7: 'If one were to give all the wealth of his house for love, it would be utterly scorned.' In Song 8:11-12 the woman is utterly rejecting the attempts of Solomon to manipulate her with money. She is forcefully declaring that her love is not for sale. One commentator effect-ively captures the essence of her mind-set in Song 8:11-12: 'If you set the price of love at a billion dollars, you would reduce it to nothing. By its very nature love must be given. Sex can be bought; but love must be given.'[3] The woman blatantly rejects all efforts to cheapen her love by putting a price on it.

> Even the richest man in the world cannot purchase true love ... True love is priceless.

In our culture, people can, and do, pay for sex, but they cannot purchase true love. Love resists being reduced to a commodity which can be trafficked. Even the richest man in the world cannot purchase true love. The Beatles got it right — money really can't buy you love. True love is priceless.

Solomon: a man who cheapened love

While it is unclear from the text of the Song of Songs whether King Solomon actually attempted to buy the woman's love, other biblical evidence regarding the life of Solomon certainly suggests that it was quite possible that he did. For instance, as we learned in the chapter on maturity, Solomon accumulated hundreds of wives and concubines (1 Kings 11:1-3). This indicates that Solomon treated women like objects, things to be possessed. Clearly, Solomon was a man who was prone to cheapen love. Therefore, it would certainly not be out of character for Solomon to actually attempt to buy the woman's love in the Song of Songs.

If Solomon did indeed try to buy her love, as is insinuated in Song of Songs 8:11-12, then we can draw three conclusions as to how he cheapened love. First, if Solomon attempted to buy the woman's love, he would have cheapened love by treating the woman as a mere object, another possession to own, control and admire — just like his vineyard. Second, if Solomon attempted to buy the woman's love, he would have cheapened love by suggesting that marriage is just like any other commercial agreement. If he indeed treated the woman like his vineyard, then he would have cheapened love by regulating his relationship with the woman according to something akin to a commercial lease or business agreement, rather than a loving covenant. Third, if Solomon attempted to buy the woman's love, he would have cheapened love through his efforts to manipulate the woman. As king of Israel, Solomon would have had tremendous power with which to leverage and force her hand, to make her love and serve him If Solomon attempted what is suggested in Song 8:11-12 then he would have cheapened love by turning it into a selfish and manipulative game.

Regardless of whether Solomon actually attempted to buy the woman's love, these verses teach us that love can be cheapened in three ways: objectification, commercialization and manipulation. These three ways of cheapening love continue to be a struggle for couples in our own day. Let's look at how each one of these errors manifests itself in modern marriages.

Objectification

The first way to cheapen love is by objectification. Objectification occurs when we treat a person of the opposite sex as an object, or possession, to be used for our own satisfaction. This is exactly what a man like Solomon might be tempted to do with the woman. As previously noted, Solomon viewed women as objects which he sought to acquire like a piece of property. In fact, there are some commentators who suggest that the vineyard Solomon speaks of in Song 8:11 is actually a metaphor for his vast harem of wives and concubines (1 Kings 11:3).[4] If this interpretation is correct, then it only bolsters the point that Solomon was prone to treat women like property and may simply have been interested in adding the woman in the Song to his vast collection. In addition, this interpretation would also suggest that Solomon viewed his harem as primarily providing him with sexual gratification because the term 'vineyard' serves as an image of female sexuality in the Song (e.g. 1:6; 2:15; & 7:8).[5] According to this metaphorical interpretation, Solomon's primary purpose in collecting women was to satisfy his lust and greed. Even if this interpretation is not correct, it is clear that Solomon viewed women in general, and perhaps the woman in the Song of Songs, as mere objects to possess for the purpose of satisfying his desires.

The nature of true love: priceless

In our culture we no longer have the practice of polygamy and we do not have harems. However, we still struggle with the problem of objectification. Today, men and women can cheapen love by engaging in the sins of prostitution and pornography. Clearly, prostitution results in the crass objectification of a person of the opposite sex. It reduces them to a piece of property which is lusted after and then acquired for money. Admittedly, most Christian men and women do not generally fall into the trap of prostitution, but the same cannot be said for the equally deadly trap of pornography.

In our day, by means of the Internet, it has become so incredibly easy to purchase love without detection. The Internet allows people to engage in objectification while avoiding the social stigma involved with prostitution. It makes the sin of sexual objectification easier to commit. However, paying to view pornography is no better than going down to the street corner and paying a prostitute for sex. In both cases love is being reduced to a commodity and a person is being bought and sold. Both pornography and prostitution reduce the image of God to an object. It is no mere coincidence that our English word 'pornography' is derived from the Greek word for 'prostitute' (porne). These joint sins of pornography and prostitution not only cheapen love by objectifying an image-bearer of God, but they also lead to other sins.

Ultimately, sexual objectification is a form of idolatry. By paying for love through prostitution or pornography we actually engage in a form of false worship. When we entangle ourselves in these sexual sins we are actually worshipping our own lustful greed and the object of our lust. This is not a new problem. In the days of the apostle Paul, many people participated in cults of prostitution wherein sex and idolatry were united. Because of this tendency, in his letters Paul frequently admonishes new Christians to separate themselves from such sexual idolatry. For example, in his letter to the Colossians the apostle issues the following command to Christians: 'Put to death, therefore, whatever belongs to your earthly nature: *sexual immorality, impurity, lust, evil desires and greed, which is idolatry'* (Colossians 3:5, emphasis mine). In these verses Paul not only relates sexual immorality to idolatry, but he also connects it to greed. At first the combination of sexual sin, idolatry and greed might strike us as odd, but, as one commentator explains, the three are fundamentally united:

> Sexual sin, greed and idolatry — what is the relation among these? Why end a list of sexual sins with an economic sin? Because sexual sin is fundamentally a matter of covetousness, an insatiable, self-gratifying greed that has *the control and consumption of the other person as its ultimate desire* (emphasis mine).[6]

Our sexual desires can become so strong that we are willing to acquire fulfilment of them just like any other material want. Sexual desire can lead us to treat a person like a product to be controlled and consumed.

Paul's admonishment in Colossians 3:5 is so timely for our own age in which pornography is ubiquitous. Michael Bentley notes the contemporary significance of Paul's command in Colossians 3:5:

> No one can say that this letter to the Colossians is 'out of date', because all around us in our world today there

are many alluring images used in advertisements, in newspapers, magazines and on television. These are designed to entice people to lust for sexual gratification. In Paul's day, the people were making an idol of sex; it is the same today. Such things amount to greed: the desire to satisfy the sinful nature, regardless of the cost or consequences.[7]

We cheapen love when we objectify people of the opposite sex through prostitution and pornography. When we allow our lust to be fuelled by greedy desire for self-satisfaction at the expense of another image-bearer of God we engage in a form of idolatry which both dishonours God and cheapens love.

Objectification of the opposite sex through prostitution and pornography not only results in idolatry, but it also destroys our union with Christ. In 1 Corinthians 6:15-16 Paul states: 'Do you not know that your bodies are members of Christ himself? Shall I then take the members of Christ and unite them with a prostitute? Never! Do you not know that he who unites himself with a prostitute is one with her in body? For it is said, "The two will become one flesh."' Paul's point here is that a Christian can either be united to Christ or united to a prostitute, but he cannot be united to both simultaneously.[8] Charles Hodge attempts to explain the meaning of these difficult verses:

> When we allow our lust to be fuelled by greedy desire for self-satisfaction at the expense of another image-bearer of God we engage in a form of idolatry.

111

That fornication is incompatible with the relation of the bodies of believers to Christ, arises out of the peculiar nature of that sin. The parties to it become partakers of a common life. Whether we can understand this or not, it is the doctrine of the Bible. Therefore as we cannot be partakers of the life of Christ, and of the life of Belial, so neither can our bodies be members of Christ, and at the same time have a common life with 'one who is a sinner', in the scriptural sense of that phrase.[9]

When you next experience the temptation to cheapen love by objectifying the image of God recall these verses to mind. Pornography and other forms of sexual immorality are not victimless sins. As we have seen in this section such sins cheapen love, distort the image of God, lead to idolatry and destroy our union with Christ. Sexual sins tear away at the very fabric of the two closest unions known to man: the union between husband and wife, and the union between God and man. Clearly, Christians must avoid cheapening love in this manner.

Commercialization

In addition to the sins of prostitution and pornography there are other more subtle ways by which couples cheapen love. One way is to commercialize it by treating the marriage covenant like a collective bargaining agreement. Solomon may have attempted to do this with the woman in the Song of Songs by treating his relationship to her like that of a landlord and tenant. Our culture also encourages us to think of the marriage covenant in a similar commercial fashion. It beckons us to view marriage as a mere legal arrangement in which the husband and wife negotiate a shared existence. This mentality often leads couples to enter into a series of orchestrated trade-offs or quid-pro-quo arrangements. When this type of crass commercialization occurs the marriage relationship looks more like a business relationship. Let me give you some examples of how couples cheapen their love through commercialization.

First, couples may commercialize their marriage by treating the allocation of household duties like a competition. Often couples begin to keep strict account of who's doing what around the house and this often leads to arguments as each begins to think he or she is doing more than his or her fair share. An illustration of this dynamic recently appeared in an article in *The Wall Street Journal*. The following account displays how a marriage can be reduced to a collective bargaining dispute over household chores:

> Bill Rogers and Joan Cummins, a Plymouth, Mich., couple, know the problem all too well. Mr. Rogers does a chunk of the housework, including shopping, weekday cooking, yard work and his own laundry, and Ms. Cummins admits she undervalues his role. But so many of the mundane tasks that must be done immediately fall to her, Ms. Cummins says, such as cleaning the kitchen, that she becomes resentful. 'It's the everyday things that get under your skin.'
>
> When she arrived home one recent day from her job as a bank vice president, she found a dishwasher full of

clean dishes needing to be put away and used cups by the sink. 'How come you didn't empty the dishwasher?' she asked Mr. Rogers, who arrives home earlier from his job as an insurance agent. 'Well, who cleaned the garage this weekend?' he replied. And their customary argument began. 'You never give me credit for anything I do,' he told her.[10]

This type of petty bickering cheapens love because it treats marriage like a business. This couple is clearly not serving one another in love, but rather they are marking off a checklist of contractual obligations. Christians must never reduce their marriage to this type of impersonal businesslike contract.

Another area where couples often turn their marriage covenant into a commercial contract is over the topic of money. It is very easy for couples to handle their finances like a business. Instead of sharing their entire lives, couples often carve out finances as an area to be handled more like a business partnership. Again a recent article in *The Wall Street Journal* illustrates well this type of mentality:

Mary Glenn readily changed her name when she got married. But though she and her husband share nearly everything and have two kids together, there's one thing Ms. Glenn will never give up: her own checking [bank] account.

Ms. Glenn splits the household expenses with her husband but keeps a separate account for her own autonomy, security and peace of mind. 'It's so freeing to be your own person, and not to feel like someone else is looking over your shoulder,' says the Colleyville, Texas, software executive.[11]

Now there are many ways for couples to arrange their finances and there is nothing inherently wrong with a spouse having a separate bank account, but when the impetus for such an arrangement is a fear that your husband won't give you 'peace' and 'security' and that he is some taskmaster who is 'looking over your shoulder' you have a problem. When couples treat their finances like a commercial business partnership they cheapen love. Christians are called to treat their marriages as covenantal unions, not business deals.

Manipulation

Finally, couples can cheapen love through manipulation. Solomon may have thought that he could manipulate the woman in the Song of Songs because he was a wealthy and powerful man. He may have been tempted to get what he wanted from her by playing his cards right. Modern couples often engage in similar forms of manipulation, but it usually takes place on a much more subtle level. For example, it is very tempting for men to take for granted, or even mistreat, their wives, and then pay them back with a material gift while never really asking for forgiveness, repenting or even dealing with the underlying problem. They manipulate their wives by paying them off and they thereby cheapen love. But women are not immune from playing manipulative games either. For instance, sometimes women use physical intimacy as a bargaining chip to get what they want from their husbands. This form of manipulation also cheapens love.

In 1 Corinthians 13:5 the apostle Paul declares that love is never 'self-seeking'. Manipulation, on the other hand, is always self-seeking. It is a means of getting what *you* want from your partner. Therefore, manipulation is in direct opposition to true love. Married couples cheapen love any time they play these selfish manipulative games. Self-seeking manipulation distorts the very heart of true love. True love does not lead to a self-seeking attitude, but rather it fosters an attitude of self-sacrifice and self-surrender. One commentator describes the core of true love as including 'the self-surrender for the good of the other, without expecting or demanding any reward. This unselfish abandonment to the other will bring its own happy and unsought for compensations.'[12] Manipulation cheapens human love because it is always motivated by a self-seeking purpose which is contrary to the very definition of love. Christians must avoid cheapening love in this manner.

Ponder the priceless nature of true love

A Christian must never treat his or her spouse like Solomon may have treated the woman in the Song of Songs. Christians must never engage in objectification, commercialization or manipulation. Instead, they are to treat love as a priceless gift to be nurtured, cultivated, served and cherished.

The Song of Songs calls us to appreciate the gift of true love by pondering its priceless nature. Let me ask you, 'When was the last time you pondered the priceless nature of true love?' As a pastor, I have occasionally witnessed the debilitating impact of marital discord. Unfortunately, I have seen homes divided with strife, and husbands and wives in warfare with one another. Often after these troubling incidents I return to the parsonage, kiss my wife and thank God for the priceless gift of true love. When was the last time you did this? We too often take the gift of true love for granted. We do not esteem it highly enough. Do you

> **Christians are to treat love as a priceless gift to be nurtured, cultivated, served and cherished.**

realize that it is truly amazing that God, in his providence, has provided you with the gift of a spouse? As the book of Proverbs declares, 'He who finds a wife finds what is good and receives favour from the LORD,' (Proverbs 18:22). Of course, the same principle is true for the woman who finds a husband! God is the giver of the gift of human love and for that reason alone we should desire to ponder its priceless nature because it reveals something about him. The Song of Songs reminds us to never treat true love as a cheap trinket or even as something we are entitled to, but rather to treat true love as a priceless gift from God.

The most priceless love of all

If you desire to come to a greater understanding regarding the priceless nature of true human love simply begin by contemplating the love of God for his people. God's love for his people is priceless. It is inestimable. The psalmist declares this in Psalm 36:7: 'How priceless is your unfailing love! Both high and low among men find refuge in the shadow of your wings.' Furthermore, God does not treat his people as objects, but rather as image-bearers. He does not treat his covenant with his people as a mere cold legal arrangement, but rather as a warm bond of love. He does not deal with his people as a party to a contract, but rather he deals with them as his beloved bride. He does not use checklists and he is not stingy with our spiritual inheritance. God is never self-seeking or manipulative. In addition, God's love can never be purchased and it can never be earned; rather it is given as a gift. As the apostle Paul notes, 'For it is by grace you have been saved, through faith — and this not from yourselves, *it is the gift of God* — not by works, so that no one can boast,' (Ephesians 2:8-9, emphasis mine). Just as the woman in the Song of Songs gave her love to the one she chose, God has also freely given his love to those he chose before the creation of the world (Ephesians 1:4-5).

Finally, God the Father has also revealed the priceless nature of love by giving the most inestimable gift of love to his people: 'For God so loved the world that he gave his one and only Son, that whoever believes in him shall not perish but have eternal life,' (John 3:16). There is nothing more priceless in this world than the broken body and shed blood of Jesus Christ. If it was absurd for Solomon to attempt to buy the woman's love for a thousand shekels of silver, how much more absurd was it for Judas to try to sell the greatest love of all for thirty shekels of silver? Judas' attempt to put a price on the greatest love of all was utterly scornful. God the Father has demonstrated to us the meaning of priceless love by giving us his only Son (1 John 3:16). Therefore, be perfect as your Heavenly Father is perfect — treat love as a priceless gift.

Questions for discussion and review

1. *Read 1 Corinthians 13. Compile a list of the attributes of love which you find in this text. Pay particular attention to attributes which connect with what we have discussed in this chapter. For example, think about how Paul speaks of the priceless nature of true love.*

2. *Examine yourself and your marriage. Make a list of ways in which you have cheapened love through objectification, commercialization or manipulation. If you have fallen in these areas, confess these sins to God and pray for forgiveness. Then begin the process of repentance by turning away from these sins. Discuss your self-assessment with your spouse.*

3. *Take some time to pray to God to thank him for the gift of your spouse. After praying, express to your spouse, either verbally or in writing, how grateful you are for them.*

4. *Contemplate the priceless nature of God's love for you by reading and reflecting on the following verses:*
   a. *Exodus 34:6*
   b. *Psalm 103:8*
   c. *Ephesians 5:1-2*
   d. *1 John 3:1*
   e. *1 John 4:7*

5. *Read and meditate on the following texts: Matthew 22:36-38; and 1 John 5:2. What do they reveal about how you are to respond to God's priceless love?*

7. Maintaining true love: foster friendship

'My lover spoke and said to me,
"Arise, my darling, my beautiful one,
and come with me,"'
(Song 2:10).

'You have stolen my heart, my sister, my bride; you have stolen
my heart with one glance of your eyes,
with one jewel of your necklace,'
(Song 4:9).

'His mouth is sweetness itself; he is altogether lovely.
This is my lover, this my friend,
O daughters of Jerusalem,'
(Song 5:16).

In our culture, we often treat love, particularly romantic
physical love, as the pinnacle of human experience. Just

consider how sexual intimacy is depicted in modern films and on television. Most of such instances in the media today treat physical intimacy as *the* goal and finale of the male/female relationship. Our culture is so obsessed with physical sexuality that it uses the word 'sex' as a synonym for love, as if the two concepts are interchangeable. Marva Dawn notes that this tendency to equate love with the physical sexual act is evidenced by how our culture uses the phrase 'make love'.[1] For most people, this is a means of referring to sexual relations. Our culture treats an act of biology as if it is the sum and substance of the meaning of human love. The modern world treats the physical sexual act as something which may be wholly disconnected from other forms of intimacy. The Bible, however, teaches a much fuller and richer view of love. Whereas our culture calls us to 'make love' independent from other forms of intimacy, the Song teaches us that lovers must also be friends. The Song of Songs reveals that true love is strengthened when couples possess and foster an intimate friendship. It tells us that making friends is part of making love.

As you read the Song of Songs you cannot help but feel the pulse of the deep friendship shared between the lovers. Their intense yearning to be alone together is not just about satisfying their physical desires; they also long to be together because they are best friends. They are true companions who are longing to share the joys of intimate friendship. The couple in the Song reveal the depth of their friendship through the terms they use to refer to each other. Let's look at how each member of the couple expresses this deep friendship. We'll begin with the woman.

My friend, my lover

In Song of Songs 5:16, the woman reveals that her relationship to the man includes a union of physical and emotional intimacy. This union is revealed through the two terms the woman employs to refer to the man in this verse: 'His mouth is sweetness itself; he is altogether lovely. *This is my lover, this is my friend*, O daughters of Jerusalem,' (emphasis mine). As you can see, the woman refers to him as both her 'lover' and her 'friend'. For the woman in the Song, physical intimacy can never be disconnected from emotional intimacy. For her, love cannot be detached from friendship. Her husband is both a lover and a friend. The fact that the woman viewed these two concepts, 'lover' and 'friend', as inextricably intertwined is bolstered by the poetic structure of this verse. Here we once again encounter the poetic device known as 'synonymous parallelism'. As we have seen, this is essentially a way of saying the same thing in two different ways. In Song 5:16 the woman uses 'lover' and 'friend' as interchangeable and synonymous terms. Whereas our culture equates love with sex, the woman in the Song of Songs equates love with friendship. In other words, she is saying that true love requires both romantic love and the love of friendship.

It is interesting to note that the Hebrew word translated as 'friend' in Song 5:16 could also legitimately be translated as 'neighbour'. In fact, the same Hebrew word is translated as 'neighbour' in Leviticus 19:18: 'Do not seek revenge or bear a grudge against one of your people, but love your *neighbour* as yourself. I am the LORD,' (emphasis mine). The Bible, in both the Old and New Testaments, calls us to love our neighbours as ourselves. It calls us to display a friendship love which seeks the best for our neighbour. Clearly, this concept of 'neighbour love' or 'friendship love' takes on a much deeper meaning when the neighbour is our spouse. The great Reformer Martin Luther commented as follows regarding the connection between the command to love our neighbour and the marriage relationship: 'Of course, the Christian should love his wife. He is supposed to love his neighbour, and since his wife is his nearest neighbour, she should be his deepest love.' The woman in the Song of Songs reminds us of this important element of true love. She reminds us that lovers must also be friends. However, the woman is not the only one who teaches us about the importance of friendship in the Song.

My darling, my sister, my bride

The man in the Song of Songs also reveals that his lover is his friend. He expresses the depth of his friendship with the woman by referring to her by two terms of endearment: his 'darling' and his 'sister'. These two terms reveal that the woman was not just his lover, but she was also his closest friend. Let's look briefly at each of these two terms used by the man in the Song.

The term of endearment most frequently employed by the man to express his friendship with the woman is 'my darling'. The man uses this designation a total of nine times in the Song of Songs (1:9; 1:15; 2:2; 2:10; 2:13; 4:1; 4:7; 5:2; and 6:4). The word 'darling' corresponds well with the word 'friend', which is the term of endearment used by the woman in Song 5:16.

In fact, the Hebrew word which is translated as 'darling' is the feminine form of the very same word which is translated as 'friend' in that verse. The man, like the woman, refers to his lover as his friend.

The man also expresses his intimate friendship with the woman through a second term of endearment: 'sister'. He uses this word a total of five times in the Song (4:9; 4:10; 4:12; 5:1; and 5:2). For example, he uses it in Song 4:9 where he declares to his love, 'You have stolen my heart, *my sister*, my bride; you have stolen my heart with one glance of your eyes, with one jewel of your necklace,' (emphasis mine). In the ancient Near East it was quite common for a husband to use the word 'sister' as a term of endearment for his wife.[2] The man considered the woman such an intimate companion that he referred to her in familial terms. She was as close to him as a sister.

In Song of Songs 5:16 we saw how the woman combined romantic love and friendship by referring to the man both as her 'lover' and 'friend'. A similar parallel combination occurs in the man's words in Song of Songs 4:9. In this verse the man refers to the woman as both his 'sister' and as his 'bride'. Here the man, just like the woman in Song 5:16, reveals that true love is built upon the twin pillars of romantic love and intimate friendship. As commentator Richard Hess notes, 'The reference to the female's role as sister and bride is intended to convey both the closeness of the brother/sister relationship and the commitment of marriage.'[3] The significance of this combination of terms ('sister' and 'bride') is further enhanced by the repetitive linkage of them in two other verses in the Song of Songs (4:10 and 4:12). The man not only desires romantic and physical intimacy with his beloved, but he also yearns for

> God has called husbands and wives to be intimate friends. The best of marriages are those between the best of friends.

her to be his most intimate companion. In other words, he longs for her to be his best friend.

Clearly, the Song of Songs teaches us that true love requires both romantic love and intimate friendship. The lovers in the Song were the closest of friends and yearned for one another's company. As Paige Patterson notes about the lovers in the Song, '...in addition to their intimate expression of affection there was also the desire simply to be together. Each doubtless had other friends, *yet their most important friendship was that between themselves*,' (emphasis mine).[4]

God has called husbands and wives to be intimate friends. The best of marriages are those between the best of friends. Therefore, it is vitally important for couples to foster friendship in their marriage. So how can couples do this? The Bible's answer is quite simple. The Bible suggests that the primary way that a husband and wife can foster friendship is by working together, side by side, in God's kingdom. In order to grasp how this principle works we must return to the Garden of Eden and the first friendship.

The first friendship

In the beginning, God placed Adam in a beautiful garden and gave him a command to 'work it and take care of it' (Genesis

2:15). This command to work is what theologians refer to as a 'creation mandate' or 'creation ordinance'. Creation mandates are principles which God wove into the very fabric of this world prior to the Fall. Creation mandates are particularly important because they represent timeless principles which are to govern our lives until the return of Christ. In other words, creation mandates are never revoked by God. Among these irrevocable commands was the command to work. God gave man work, not as a curse, but as a central part of his plan for this world. Perhaps you are asking yourself, 'What does the creation mandate to work have to do with fostering friendship in the marriage relationship?' In order to answer that question we must look at what occurred on Adam's first day of work.

Adam's first day on the job

Interestingly, the first specific enumerated task God gave to Adam was naming the animals: 'Now the LORD God had formed out of the ground all the beasts of the field and all the birds of the air. *He brought them to the man to see what he would name them*; and whatever the man called each living creature, that was its name,' (Genesis 2:19, emphasis mine). What an overwhelming task! Why did God give it to Adam? I think it was for two reasons. First, God assigned Adam the task of naming the animals in order to demonstrate to him that he was called to rule the earth in conjunction with God. He was to be God's vicegerent. However, there was a second reason why God assigned Adam this task and it directly relates to the issue of fostering friendship in marriage. God wanted Adam

Called to be co-labourers

It is important to recognize that Adam's primary concern was finding a helper suitable to him and not just someone with whom he could be physically intimate. He wasn't looking primarily for a biological companion, but rather he was looking for a helper and a counterpart.[6] He was looking for someone who would work with him to fulfil his God-ordained tasks. In Eve, in his wife, he found this fellow worker. He now had a co-labourer who would join him in accomplishing the great mandate conveyed by God in Genesis 1:28: 'God blessed them and said to them, "Be fruitful and increase in number; fill the earth and subdue it. Rule over the fish of the sea and the birds of the air and over every living creature that moves on the ground."' Adam, with Eve at his side, was now ready to engage God's world. He was ready to work. Adam and Eve were ready to embark on fulfilling Genesis 1:28 *together*.

It is important for couples to take note of the calling God gave Adam and Eve in Genesis 1:28 because this command is a creation mandate and, therefore, it remains in effect for couples today. In Genesis 1:28, God revealed that marriage is not only for procreation ('Be fruitful and increase in number'), but is also for subduing and ruling the earth ('Fill the earth and subdue it. Rule over the fish of the sea and the birds of the air and over every living creature that moves on the ground'). Therefore, from the very beginning, God revealed that the marriage relationship is not just about physical intimacy. Marriage, according to God, is also about working together. Genesis reveals that husbands and wives are companions and partners in the great task of bringing God's glory to every sphere of his created world. Husbands and wives are called to be co-labourers in God's kingdom. They are called to work together. Biblical scholar Andreas Köstenberger notes that this marital togetherness is absolutely central to fulfilling the mandate of Genesis 1:28: '*Together* they are to execute it according to the will and for the glory of God. *Together* they are to multiply and be stewards of the children given to them by God. And *together* they are to subdue the earth…'[7]

I believe that the togetherness experienced by couples as they work together in God's kingdom is essential for fostering friendship. When couples work together they are exploring the core of their companionship. By engaging God's world together, couples can forge an intimacy by rediscovering who they were created to be and how they were created to relate to one another. Couples can foster friendship by working together as God intended.

> …husbands and wives are companions and partners in the great task of bringing God's glory to every sphere of his created world.

Fostering friendship by working together as God intended

It is crucial for couples to remember that God did not give work to Adam and Eve as a punishment or a burden. Rather, he gave them this work as a blessing and an opportunity to

131

explore their companionship. Unfortunately, too many couples in our culture fail to view their marital co-labouring as a blessing, let alone as an opportunity to become better friends. Modern couples are often unable to work together effectively, and some find absolutely no joy in working together. In fact, many spouses are filled with dread even about the prospect of working with their mate. This type of thinking is wholly contrary to God's plan for marriage. Christian couples must not adopt the mindset of the world when it comes to working together. So how can couples avoid these errors? How can couples make working together as husband and wife the joy it was intended to be? How can couples use their co-labouring to foster friendship? Let me suggest three steps which couples can take to foster friendship through sharing their work.

Step 1: Expand your definition of 'making love'

First, couples must begin simply by expanding their definition of the phrase 'to make love'. As noted in the beginning of this chapter, our modern culture relegates this phrase solely to the realm of sexual relations. However, as we have seen from both the Song of Songs and Genesis, love is also made as couples work together as husband and wife. Couples must begin to value their opportunities to work together and view them as 'making love'. Marva Dawn calls couples to recognize this more capacious view of making love by noting that:

> Love is made all the time in a marriage — when together we clean up the kitchen, sing a hymn side by side in a worship service, ride our bicycles to the neighbourhood

park, talk on the porch swing about the day's work, play a game, plan for the future, or remember the past.[8]

Christian couples must avoid falling into the thinking patterns of the world. They must not value the sexual act more highly than the cultivation of friendship. Whereas our culture suggests that erotic love is to be more prized than friendship, the Song tells us they are of equal value. C. S. Lewis also argued that erotic love must be conjoined with friendship. He contended that friendship is a love which is 'even as great a love as Eros'.[9] Lewis proved his point by posing the following hypothetical question:

> Suppose you are fortunate enough to have 'fallen in love with' and married your Friend. And now suppose it possible that you were offered the choice of two futures: '*Either* you two will cease to be lovers but remain forever joint seekers of the same God, the same beauty, the same truth, *or else*, losing all that, you will retain as long as you live the raptures and ardours, all the wonder and the wild desire of Eros. Choose which you please.' Which should we choose? Which choice should we not regret after we had made it?[10]

Do you see Lewis' point? Can you imagine having to choose between your spouse being *either* your lover *or* your friend? What an awful dilemma! True love involves both romance and friendship. Thankfully, the Song reminds us that we do not have to make a choice between the two; we are to experience both.

Couples must think biblically about making love. They must value friendship as much as physical intimacy. In other words, couples must come to value an intimate walk in the park as highly as an intimate night in the bedroom. Couples can foster friendship by expanding their definition of what it means to 'make love'.

Step 2: Play together

Second, couples can also foster friendship by playing together. Married people should spend time playing, relaxing and recreating together. Engaging in these activities is a form of co-labouring; it is a form of work. At first this may sound counterintuitive because in our culture we so often treat playing, or recreation, as the opposite of work. In our society, work is viewed as burdensome labour which we do in an office, cubicle or factory; and recreation is an enjoyable activity that we engage in during our leisure time. The Bible does not reflect this modern work/recreation distinction. As we have already noted, the Bible views work as a blessing, rather than a burden. It also has an expansive view of work. Essentially, the Bible calls us to serve God, or work for him, in everything we do. This mindset is reflected in Paul's words in 1 Corinthians 10:31: 'So whether you eat or drink or *whatever you do*, do it all for the glory of God,' (emphasis mine). Therefore, our leisure activities are also something we *do* for the glory of God. According to the Bible, playing *is* part of our work.

Because recreation is a form of work, couples can grow closer by engaging in it. In other words, couples are called not only to work together, but also to play together. Therefore, it is helpful for couples to foster their friendship by developing common interests. In fact, one of the pillars of an enduring friendship is the sharing of common interests. C. S. Lewis comments on this dynamic:

> Friendship arises out of mere companionship when two or more of the companions discover they have in common some insight or interest or even taste which the others do not share and which, till that moment, each believed to be his own unique treasure (or burden). The typical expression of opening Friendship would be something like, 'What? You too? I thought I was the only one.'[11]

Couples can foster friendship by jointly engaging in hobbies and other forms of leisure activities. Therefore, make an effort to get involved in the interests of your spouse.

Involving yourself in what interests your spouse not only fosters friendship by allowing you to spend time together, but it also helps you to get to know your spouse better. If your spouse really loves to do something it is likely that this activity reveals much about who they are as a person. For example, my wife loves to engage in a hobby known as 'scrapbooking'. Scrapbooking involves placing photographs on custom-made pages which are extremely decorative and detailed. It can take her hours to make one page. Frankly, I have no interest in directly participating in this hobby at all. However, I have learned to become interested in it, and to encourage her in it, because I recognize how much it means to her and what it reveals about her. My wife engages in scrapbooking because she cares about the life we have forged together as husband and wife. She desires to chronicle and preserve our memories through her hobby. By involving myself in her hobby, even in limited ways such as buying her scrapbooking items or looking with genuine interest at her completed pages, I have learned not only how creative my wife is, but how much she cares about our marriage and family. Understanding her interest in scrapbooking has helped me to understand her. By displaying interest in your spouse's hobbies you demonstrate to them that you care about what they care about and that you want to get to know them better.

It is too often the case that couples fail to set aside time for joint recreation. Modern couples often work together in the more mundane tasks of daily life, but when it comes time to play, to have fun, they often leave one another and engage in these activities with their 'friends'. This type of segregation does not foster marital intimacy. In fact, it can actually erode your relationship because it can lead to a subconscious conclusion that your spouse is the person with whom you do the tedious stuff and your 'friends' are those with whom you have fun. Don't make this mistake. Make sure that you both work and play with your *best* friend. Friendship is fostered when couples play together.

Step 3: Make your work a labour of love

Third, it is vital that couples deliberately utilize their work as an opportunity to get to know one another better. My point here is that it is not enough just to complete a task together. Couples must use the task as an opportunity for mutual exploration and discovery. If couples work together in silence then their work will not likely foster a deeper friendship. Therefore, use your work as an opportunity to talk. Most tasks, particularly menial tasks, offer a great opportunity for spouses to communicate. This communication not only enhances the marital relationship, but it also helps the work go faster!

This may at first seem like a simple principle, but do not underestimate its importance and rewards. R. C. Sproul provides this helpful reminder regarding the blessings and benefits of getting to know your spouse: 'To make a conscious effort to gain insight into a human being is not simply a sober responsibility in marriage, but a very special privilege. Few areas of study can be so exciting and fruitful. If it is a labour of love, that love will only be intensified.'[12] I have been married to my wife for twelve years and I still discover new things about her. Often I make these discoveries in the midst of the most mundane tasks such as clearing the dishes from the kitchen table or changing our child's nappy. When I learn something new about my wife I feel much like a miner who has just found a gold nugget. Remember to make your work a labour of love by deliberately using the time as an opportunity to foster friendship with your spouse.

Aquila and Priscilla: lovers, friends and co-labourers

The main point of this chapter is that married couples must be both lovers and friends and that marital friendship is particularly fostered as spouses work together in God's kingdom. The New Testament provides a wonderful example of a couple who exemplified this pattern of working together as husband and wife. The couple to which I am referring is Aquila and Priscilla.

In Aquila and Priscilla we see a couple working together, side by side, to glorify God in his kingdom. They worked together in a seemingly mundane task, tent making, in order to benefit the church (Acts 18:2-3). In addition, Aquila and Priscilla jointly served as missionaries alongside the apostle Paul (Acts 18:18-19). This couple also co-laboured in exercising hospitality. For example, the Bible tells us that Aquila and Priscilla opened their home to host the church when they lived in Ephesus (1 Corinthians 16:19) and when they lived in Rome (Romans 16:3-5). Finally, the couple also worked together to honour God by correcting and refining the theological understanding of a gifted young preacher named Apollos (Acts 18:26).

Aquila and Priscilla worked together in a variety of ways, as both lovers and friends, to honour and glorify God. They glorified God in both the more mundane tasks of life (i.e. tent making and hospitality) and the adventurous tasks as well (i.e. missionary journey and theological instruction). Although the Bible does not give us a great amount of detail about their relationship, it is safe for us to infer from the fact that they are always mentioned together that they enjoyed both a close companionship and actually working together. Aquila and Priscilla provide an excellent example of how marital co-labouring can not only build the bonds of friendship, but also build God's kingdom and glorify him.

As I conduct premarital counselling I try to emphasize to young couples that marriage is an awesome opportunity to glorify God. I try to get them to see that this is the ultimate purpose of marriage. I often illustrate this point by telling them about how ancient Near Eastern kings would set up statues bearing their image within the bounds of their territory to remind those who lived there that the king was sovereign over that territory.[13] Even though the king was not physically present, his image served as a reminder of his rule. God accomplishes a similar thing by placing his image in the territory over which he is sovereign — the entire earth! The Bible defines God's image as follows: 'So God created man in his own image, in the image of God he created him; *male and female he created them,'* (Genesis 1:27, emphasis mine). As married couples work together in a manner which glorifies God they are not only forging a deeper friendship, but they are also bearing God's kingly image to a watching world. Aquila and Priscilla bore God's image well. How about you and your marriage? What does your marriage say to a watching world?

> As married couples work together in a manner which glorifies God they are not only forging a deeper friendship, but they are also bearing God's kingly image to a watching world.

The model of loving friendship

While this chapter includes a few helpful suggestions which will aid couples in fostering friendship, the most important step in this process is recognizing the greatest friendship of all. In order to foster a greater friendship with your spouse you must first appreciate the loving friendship which God has established with his people. God's establishes the model of loving friendship which we should endeavour to emulate in our marriages. The Bible reveals that God is not only our king, but he is also our companion. God is our most intimate, closest and best friend. He reveals the depth of his friendship with his people by calling them to co-labour with him and by giving them his one and only Son.

Do you realize that God has called his people to work with him to fulfil his redemptive plan? Obviously, he does not need us in order to bring his plan to fruition, but he has chosen to use us as vessels to achieve his ends. He chose to make us co-labourers with him from the very beginning. For example, as we saw in this chapter, God placed man in his garden and told him to cultivate it, tend it and keep it. He called Adam and Eve to be co-stewards and co-rulers of his world. Just as God worked to create the world, he also calls man, as his image bearer, to work in the creation. He has called his people to co-labour with him to achieve his glorious purposes and also to grow.

This dynamic of divine co-labouring is also present in the New Testament. Think about how Christ began his earthly ministry. He gathered men to work with him. He called a core group of close friends, his apostles, to labour with him side by side. He turned a fisherman like Peter into a fisher of men. He informs these apostles in Acts 1:8 that they will continue this co-labouring after he has ascended to heaven by declaring that they will be his 'witnesses'. Christ also informs the church that this co-labouring will continue after the apostolic age and will last until the end of this age:

> Then Jesus came to them and said, 'All authority in heaven and on earth has been given to me. *Therefore go and make disciples of all nations, baptizing them in the name of the Father and of the Son and of the Holy Spirit, and teaching them to obey everything I have commanded you. And surely I am with you always, to the very end of the age,'*
> (Matthew 28:18-20, emphasis mine).

Our faithful co-labouring with God not only leads to the fulfilment of his will, but it also allows us to grow closer to him. This pattern should be emulated in our marriages. As we work together as husband and wife we must always remember that we are thereby imitating the pattern of our God who calls us to co-labour with him.

Finally, God the Father also expressed the depth of his friendship with his people by giving them Jesus. Roger Ellsworth, in his Christological commentary on the Song of Songs, properly declares that, 'Out of all the special friendships most of us enjoy, none can compare with the friendship of the Lord Jesus Christ.'[14] Jesus is our closest and most dear friend. He refers to us as his friends. As Ellsworth points out, just prior to his crucifixion, Jesus spoke these words to his disciples, 'Greater love has no one than this, that he lay down his life for his friends,' (John 15:13). We are Christ's modern-day disciples. We are those for whom Christ laid down his life. We are the friends of Jesus Christ. He is our best friend who sticks closer to us than a brother (Proverbs 18:24). Therefore, imitate Christ in your marriage by fostering a deep friendship with your spouse.

Questions for review and discussion

1. *Discuss ways in which our culture has exalted erotic and romantic love over other forms of love. Search yourself to see if you have adopted the mindset of our culture on this issue. For example, ask yourself the following question: 'Are my expectations for marriage derived from the Bible or from the godless culture in which I live?'*

2. *Make a short list of your spouse's interests and hobbies. Think about ways in which you can become more involved in these things. Also, make a short list of potential new activities which you can engage in together. Make a commitment to engage in an area of common interest this month.*

3. *Examine yourself to see if you have been fostering your friendship with God. Are you taking seriously your obligation to co-labour with him in his kingdom? Do you long for communion with him?*

4. *In this chapter, I used Aquila and Priscilla as an example of how spouses can foster their friendship and glorify God by working together in his kingdom. However, the Bible also reveals that spouses can work together effectively and yet not honour God. Read Acts 5:1-11 and discuss how Ananias and Sapphira work together as a couple to dishonour God. Can you think of other marriages in the Bible that were dishonouring to God like the marriage of Ananias and Sapphira? (See 1 Kings 21 and Mark 6:17-28.)*

8. Maintaining true love: complement one another

The Song of Hiawatha

As unto the bow the cord is,
So unto the man is woman;
Though she bends him, she obeys him,
Though she draws him, yet she follows.
(Henry Wadsworth Longfellow)

♦ ♦ ♦ ♦

'Who is this coming up from the desert leaning on her lover?'
(Song of Songs 8:5).

When I was twelve years old, I played the trumpet for a period of about two weeks. The reason I quit after only two weeks was that I quickly realized I couldn't keep a tune to save my life! In fact, I was so musically challenged that my music teacher consistently designated me to play the triangle or the wood block. However, even these simple instruments often proved too complex for me. I frequently struck them at the wrong time. When it came to music class, I was always off key and I always stuck out like a sore thumb.

Nothing is more destructive to the beauty of a musical performance than when one member plays the wrong note or sings off key, like I did in my sixth grade music class. Disharmony and dissonance always stand out. Something similar to these can occur in the marital relationship. In some ways marriage is analogous to a musical performance; it can be marked by harmony or disharmony. There are some couples who make beautiful music together and there are others who simply make noise.

When married couples function harmoniously they faithfully reflect the image of God. After all, God is a God of harmony. His creation, although vast and diverse, sings one harmonious tune. He created the world with a variety of complementary relationships such as light and darkness, morning and evening, and sea and dry land. He also created humanity in a complementary relationship. He created humanity both male and female. Just like the rest of creation, the union of male and female in marriage is meant to exhibit the harmony and order which is inherent in God himself. Therefore, when couples function harmoniously they join the chorus of the heavens in declaring the glory of

> ...when couples function harmoniously they join the chorus of the heavens in declaring the glory of God.

144

God. God created husbands and wives to make beautiful music together. He created them to complement one another.

Created to complement

In Genesis 1:27 we learn that men and women are 'hard-wired' to complement one another: 'So God created man in his own image, in the image of God he created him; *male and female he created them*,' (Genesis 1:27, emphasis mine). When God created man he made him both 'male and female'. This verse not only reveals the sexual distinction present in humanity, it also points to something much deeper about humanity. This verse teaches us that humanity is incomplete without fellowship and interaction with other humans. As theologian Anthony Hoekema notes, 'What is being said in this verse is that the human person is not an isolated being who is complete in himself or herself, but that he or she is a being who needs the fellowship of others, who is not complete apart from others.'[1] All humans have an innate need to participate in a social web of complementary relationships. This universal need becomes particularly significant in the closest of all human relationships — marriage. The book of Genesis reveals how this need emerged in the first marriage.

In Genesis 2:18, God ordains marriage by declaring that: 'It is not good for the man to be alone. I will make a helper suitable for him.' When God gave Adam a wife he gave him someone who was 'suitable for him'. He gave him a match who completed him. He gave Adam a complement. Eve contributed something to Adam's existence which he lacked without her. Genesis 2:18 sets forth a principle which applies to all marriages. It reveals something about every union of male and female. It teaches us that every marriage union is greater than the sum of its parts. Again, Anthony Hoekema provides some helpful theological reflection as he draws the following conclusions from Genesis 2:18 regarding the complementary relationship between man and woman:

> ...woman complements man, supplements him, completes him, is strong where he may be weak, supplies his deficiencies and fills his need. Man is therefore incomplete without woman. This holds for the woman as well as for the man. Woman, too, is incomplete without the man; man supplements the woman, complements her, fills her needs, is strong where she is weak.[2]

According to Genesis, men and women were created to complement one another. Like two adjoining pieces of a puzzle they were meant to become something greater together than they were when they existed apart.

How should couples complement one another?

Now that we have established that men and women were created to complement one another the question naturally arises, 'How should they complement one another in the marriage relationship?' Admittedly, it is very difficult to describe all the possible ways husbands and wives can complement each other. After all, every couple represents a union of two unique individuals possessing different gifts. Sometimes Christians erroneously attempt to suggest that all couples should complement each other in the exact same way. They normally make this error by forcing husbands and wives to fit rigid gender stereotypes which are often not biblically based at all. Christians are particularly prone to do this in the area of the division of labour between husband and wife. Biblical scholar Andreas Köstenberger reminds Christians to not equate 'traditional' cultural gender roles with biblical mandates:

> Traditional marriage may be understood as the type of division of labour by which women are responsible for cooking, cleaning, doing the laundry, and so on, while men are at work earning the family income. While Scripture does specify work outside the home as men's primary sphere and the home as the centre of the women's activity (e.g., Gen. 3:16-19; Prov. 31:10-31 [though the women's reach is not *limited* to the home]; 1 Tim. 2:15; 5:10, 14), the Bible is not a law book and does not seek to legislate the exact division of labour husband and wife ought to observe.[3]

One example cited by Köstenberger to prove his claim is that Abraham (Genesis 18:1-8), Lot (Genesis 19:3) and Esau (Genesis 27:30-31) all engaged in meal preparation, a task that we often associate solely with women.[4] The point is that we must be careful not to make biblical laws out of cultural preferences and conditions.

The Song of Songs also serves to debunk many traditional gender stereotypes. For example, the woman is the lead character in this book. She speaks more often than the man. One scholar has noted that the woman's voice constitutes 53% of the Song of Songs whereas all the male voices constitute only 34%.[5] In addition, the woman in the Song takes the initiative in the romantic relationship more frequently than her husband. For example, the woman takes the initiative at least thirteen times in the Song (1:2; 1:4; 1:7; 2:17; 3:1; 3:2; 4:16; 5:5; 7:11; 7:12; 8:1; 8:5; 8:14) while the man takes the initiative only six times (2:4; 2:10; 2:14; 4:8; 5:2; 7:8).[6] Again, this should lead us to be cautious when we approach the topic of gender roles and how spouses are to complement one another.

While it is important to caution against biblically unwarranted generalizations, the Bible does give us one clear universal pattern regarding how spouses are to complement one another. The Bible unequivocally mandates that a husband is called to lead his wife and a wife is called to submit to her husband's Christ-like leadership. We see this pattern displayed metaphorically in the Song of Songs.

Leaning on her lover

In the Song of Songs the two lovers make beautiful music together. They are in perfect harmony and enjoy complementing one another. This harmonic relationship is depicted wonderfully in the first part of Song of Songs 8:5. In that verse, the daughters of Jerusalem see the lovers approaching them and inquire, 'Who is this coming up from the desert leaning on her lover?' Here the lovers are seen walking together in harmony and their posture reveals the depth of this harmony. As they walk, the woman leans on her lover and he, in turn,

148

embraces and supports her. Their posture reveals that they are in tune with the most fundamental way that husbands and wives are to complement one another. He leads and she leans. He guides and she follows. He supports and she rests upon him. One commentator notes that the image of Song 8:5 '...captures the gracious leadership exercised by the man and the joyful acceptance of it by the woman'.[7] In essence, Song 8:5 displays metaphorically and pictorially the substance of what the apostle Paul teaches about the interrelationship of husband and wife in Ephesians 5:22-25:

> Wives, submit to your husbands as to the Lord. For the husband is the head of the wife as Christ is the head of the church, his body, of which he is the Saviour. Now as the church submits to Christ, so also wives should submit to their husbands in everything. Husbands, love your wives, just as Christ loved the church and gave himself up for her.

The lovers in the Song of Songs demonstrate that they grasp the fundamental biblical principle that every husband is called to lovingly lead his wife and every wife is called to joyfully submit to her husband's loving leadership. Let's explore this fundamental complementary relationship in more detail.

The husband's contribution: leading in love

The Bible informs us that husbands are called to lead in the marital relationship. A husband complements his wife when he takes seriously his responsibility to be the covenant leader of

149

his home. We see this principle of male covenantal leadership established in the very first marriage. There are two ways by which Genesis reveals that Adam was the covenant leader of his marriage.

First, Adam's covenantal leadership is revealed by the very order of creation — Adam was formed first. The fact that Adam was created first suggests his leadership role. This conclusion is confirmed in the New Testament. For example, the apostle Paul uses the order of creation as a proof of male leadership in the church: 'I do not permit a woman to teach or to have authority over a man; she must be silent. *For Adam was formed first, then Eve,*' (1 Timothy 2:12-13, emphasis mine). Paul makes a similar point in 1 Corinthians 11:8-9: 'For man did not come from woman, but woman from man; neither was man created for woman, but woman for man.'

In addition to the order of creation, Genesis reveals that Adam was the covenantal leader of his marriage by the fact that God held Adam *primarily* accountable for what occurred in the Fall. For example, it is noteworthy that after the Fall God first confronted Adam and not Eve, even though Eve was also culpable: 'But the LORD God called *to the man*, "Where are you?"' (Genesis 3:9, emphasis mine). Although Eve was responsible for her actions before God, Adam was *primarily* accountable for what had occurred in his marriage.

Genesis reveals that the husband is the leader in the marriage relationship. Like the man in the Song of Songs, he must set the course and gently guide his wife. This creation design is not just an Old Testament concept, it continues for Christians today under the New Covenant. For example, the apostle Paul reiterates the same principle in Ephesians 5:23:

'*For the husband is the head of the wife* as Christ is the head of the church, his body, of which he is the Saviour,' (emphasis mine). Husbands must lead their wives in love.

The effects of the Fall

While the husband is called to lead in the marriage relationship, we know that men are fallen and sinful creatures. Therefore, men often fail to lead as they should. As a consequence of the Fall, the leadership of husbands is perverted. This perversion usually manifests itself in one of two ways. First, men are prone to pervert their calling to lead by not leading at all, by completely abdicating their leadership role. Second, they pervert their calling to lead by becoming tyrants. John Piper comments on this dual threat which all men face:

> Some have neglected their wives and squandered their time in front of the television or putzing around the garage or going away too often with the guys to hunt or fish or bowl. Others have been too possessive, harsh, domineering, and belittling, giving the impression through act and innuendo that wives are irresponsible or foolish.[8]

So how do men avoid these errors? Piper suggests that men must lead with 'mature masculinity'. He describes mature masculinity as follows: 'At the heart of mature masculinity is a sense of benevolent responsibility to lead, provide for and protect women in ways appropriate to a man's differing relationships.'[9] Piper expands on the meaning of 'mature masculinity' by providing the following series of biblically based propositions:

1. 'Mature masculinity expresses itself not in the demand to be served, but in the strength to serve and to sacrifice for the good of woman.'
2. 'Mature masculinity does not assume the authority of Christ over woman, but advocates it.'
3. 'Mature masculinity does not presume superiority, but mobilizes the strengths of others.'
4. 'Mature masculinity does not have to initiate every action, but feels the responsibility to provide a general pattern of initiative.'
5. 'Mature masculinity accepts the burden of the final say in disagreements between husband and wife, but does not presume to use it in every instance.'
6. 'Mature masculinity expresses its leadership in romantic sexual relations by communicating an aura of strong and tender pursuit.'[10]
7. 'Mature masculinity expresses itself in a family by taking the initiative in disciplining the children when both parents are present and a family standard has been broken.'
8. 'Mature masculinity is sensitive to cultural expressions of masculinity and adapts to them (where no sin is involved) in order to communicate to a woman that a man would like to relate not in any aggressive or perverted way, but with maturity and dignity as a man.'
9. 'Mature masculinity recognizes that the call to leadership is a call to repentance and humility and risk-taking.'[11]

We see the substance of Piper's concept of 'mature masculinity' revealed in the posture of the lovers in Song of Songs 8:5. There the husband lovingly leads his wife with 'mature masculinity'. He does not abdicate his role, but neither does he lead harshly. He guides his wife while gently embracing her. He leads her in love.

Not just leading, but leading in love

It is vitally important for husbands to remember that the Bible not only commands them to lead, but it also commands them to 'love' their wives (Ephesians 5:25), not to be 'harsh' with them (Col. 3:19) and to be 'considerate' to them (1 Peter 3:7). It is not just about leading; it is about leading in love. The Puritan Matthew Henry calls on men to remember that male leadership does not provide a licence for male tyranny. Henry proves his point by noting how Eve was created in relation to Adam. He states that Eve was 'not made out of his head to top him, not out of his feet to be trampled upon by him, but out of his side to be equal with him'.[12] Like the man in the Song of Songs, a husband must lead his wife with her at his side, not under his thumb. It is vital that husbands recognize their propensity to fail to lead their wives in a loving way through abdication or tyranny.

So how can a husband assess if he is leading in a loving way? The Bible

> Like the man in the Song of Songs, a husband must lead his wife with her at his side, not under his thumb.

provides husbands with two helpful tests to evaluate whether they are exercising loving leadership in their marriage. I refer to these as the 'Ephesians 5:25 Test' and the 'Ephesians 5:28 Test'. Both tests are relatively short, but they are both extremely challenging.

The 'Ephesians 5:25 Test'

The 'Ephesians 5:25 Test' requires that a husband continually ask himself if he is fulfilling the spirit and substance of the command set forth in that text. Ephesians 5:25 commands the following of husbands: 'Husbands, love your wives, just as Christ loved the church and gave himself up for her.' A husband must ask himself, 'Does my leadership of my wife and my home express the self-sacrificing spirit of Christ or a spirit of selfishness? Am I giving myself for my wife spiritually, materially, emotionally and sexually? Am I loving my wife like Christ loved the church?'

The 'Ephesians 5:28 Test'

The 'Ephesians 5:28 Test' calls upon a husband to repeatedly ask himself if he is fulfilling the spirit and substance of the command set forth in Ephesians 5:28: 'In this same way, husbands ought to love their wives as their own bodies. He who loves his wife loves himself.' According to this test a husband must ask himself, 'Is my leadership being expressed in such a way that it is oriented to achieving the best for my wife or the best for me? Am I leading my home in such a way to promote my wife's spiritual maturity, health, beauty, peace and well-being?'

The practical aspects of leading in love

Now that we have a better grasp of the nature of loving leadership, let us look at some of the practical aspects regarding how a husband is to lovingly lead his wife. The Bible reveals that it is essential that husbands lead in these areas of his marriage:

1. *A husband must be the spiritual leader of his home.* For example, husbands should take the initiative in establishing and leading family devotions. The husband should also lead in the choice of a church. This requirement to be a spiritual leader means that men must become students of God's Word and students of theology.

2. *A husband must be the material leader of his home.* This does not mean that a wife can never work outside the home or earn more money than her husband; it simply means that a wife should not be expected to do these things. If there is a material need in the home, it is ultimately the husband's responsibility to provide it.

3. *A husband must lead in making the tough calls.* While most decisions in a marriage should be made together by the couple, there are some issues which will require the husband to step forward and make the call. It has not happened often in my own marriage, but there have been times when my wife has looked to me and said essentially, 'This is your call. I need you to make this decision.' Husbands are the final arbiter of the tough decisions. They cannot pass the buck.

4. *A husband should lead the couple romantically.* He should make sure that his wife's needs, both physically and emotionally, are being met. This does not mean that a wife must be passive in matters of romance, but it does mean that the husband is primarily responsible for making sure that this area of the marriage is cultivated and nurtured.

5. *A husband should lead in instructing and disciplining the children.* While couples engage in many aspects of childrearing together, the husband has a unique obligation to lead in the areas of instruction and discipline. He must not leave his wife to bear these responsibilities on her own.

As a pastor I am frequently called upon to perform weddings. My pastoral oversight of a wedding not only includes pre-marital counselling and the wedding ceremony itself, but also the wedding rehearsal. I have learned one thing about conducting wedding rehearsals — someone must take charge or there will be mass chaos. A similar dynamic occurs in the context of a marriage. In order to avoid chaos, someone has to lead in the marriage relationship and God has revealed that the man was created to fulfil that role. This is a creation norm built into our first parents, into every male and female, and into the fabric of our world. In order for there to be marital harmony, in order for a husband to complement his wife, he must take the role of a loving leader in the marriage relationship. Now let us turn to see how a wife complements her husband's loving leadership.

The wife's contribution: leaning in love

The main word which describes how a wife complements her husband is 'submission'. Like the woman in the Song of Songs, a wife is to lean submissively on her husband's loving leadership. I realize that the word 'submission' often strikes fear into the hearts of many women, particularly young women in our culture. This is understandable given the failure of men to lead in a loving, Christ-like manner. My hope is that this fear will be abated by reflecting on what biblical submission really means, and what it does *not* mean.

First, let me begin by demonstrating that submission is not just a calling for wives. Every Christian is called to submit in some sphere of their life. For example, note the following:

1. *All Christians are to submit to God:* 'Submit yourselves, then, to God. Resist the devil, and he will flee from you,' (James 4:7, emphasis mine).

2. *All Christians are to submit to one another:* 'Submit to one another* out of reverence for Christ,' (Ephesians 5:21, emphasis mine).

3. *All Christian young people are called to submit to those who are older:* 'Young men, in the same way *be submissive to those who are older*' (1 Peter 5:5, emphasis mine).

4. *All Christians are called to submit to civil government:* '*Everyone must submit* himself to the governing authorities,' (Romans 13:1, emphasis mine).

5. *All Christian workers are to submit to their employers:* 'Teach slaves *to be subject* to their masters in everything, to try to please them, not to talk back to them,' (Titus 2:9, emphasis mine).

6. *All Christians are called to submit to their elders:* 'Obey your leaders and *submit to their authority*,' (Hebrews 13:17, emphasis mine).

From this short list it is abundantly clear that submission is part and parcel of being a Christian. It is not some form of punishment imposed upon wives, but rather it is a core aspect of the Christian life. Submission is as common to the Christian life as is worship, prayer and Bible reading. The fact that submission is a central part of what it means to be a Christian should remove some of the fear regarding this concept.

Second, submission is something Jesus himself exercised. The earthly life and ministry of Jesus Christ epitomized the heart of biblical submission. For example, note the following ways in which Jesus submitted himself:

1. *Jesus submitted himself in his incarnation and earthly ministry:* The apostle Paul notes the following regarding Jesus: 'Who, being in very nature God, did not consider equality with God something to be grasped, *but made himself nothing, taking the very nature of a servant,* being made in human likeness,' (Philippians 2:6-7, emphasis mine).

2. *Jesus submitted himself to the ignominious death of the cross:* In the Garden of Gethsemane Jesus prayed, 'My Father,

158

if it is possible, may this cup be taken from me. *Yet not as I will, but as you will,'* (Matthew 26:39, emphasis mine).

3. Jesus submitted himself to the entire plan of redemption: In his high priestly prayer, when he was on the verge of going to the cross, Jesus prayed the following to the Father: 'I have brought you glory on earth by completing the work *you gave me to do,'* (John 17:4, emphasis mine).

Clearly, submission is a Christ-like act. Knowing that our Lord's life was dominated by this calling should also serve to reduce the fear that often surrounds this concept.

Third, let me continue to alleviate the common fears regarding the idea of submission by making it clear what submission does *not* mean. It does *not* mean that a wife is called to obey her husband like a child. The Bible calls on children to 'obey', but it calls wives to 'submit'. These are significantly different callings. Submission also does *not* mean that a wife is to submit in all circumstances. The Bible teaches that she is called to submit 'as to the Lord' (Ephesians 5:22) and as is 'fitting in the Lord' (Colossians 3:18). This means that a woman is really ultimately submitting to Christ in her marriage. Therefore, she is not required to submit to her husband if he is being abusive to her or is calling her to submit to something which is contrary to Christ's command. Furthermore, submission is *not* a call for a wife to become a doormat nor is it a call for her to cease having her own mind. A godly wife is called upon to guide, assist and influence her husband in family decision-making. Finally, submission is *not* something that a husband imposes on his wife, but rather it is a calling which comes to the wife directly from God. It is God who commands wives to submit, not their husbands. Andreas Köstenberger provides this helpful summary regarding what biblical submission is *not*:

> The kind of submission Scripture is talking about is not akin to *slavery* where one person owns another. It is not *subservience* where one person is doing the bidding of another without intelligent input or interaction. It is not even truly *hierarchical*, since this conjures up notions of a military-style, top-down chain of command in which the soldier is asked to obey, no-questions-asked, the orders of his superior.[13]

Understanding what biblical submission does *not* mean should serve to reduce the fear, trepidation and misconceptions surrounding this concept.

Defining submission

Thus far we have seen that submission is a calling for every Christian, that it was engaged in by Jesus himself, and that it does not require wives to obey like children or to submit to their husbands' will in all circumstances. All of these serve to put the submission of the wife in its proper context, but they do not help us arrive at a concrete definition of wifely submission. So let us try to define the essence of biblical submission.

The best and most concise definition of submission I have found is from Wayne Grudem who defines submission as 'an inner quality of gentleness that affirms the leadership of the husband'.[14] As you can see from that definition submission is first and foremost an inner attitude which ultimately manifests itself in outward conduct. Because submission is essentially an attitude it is impossible to describe exactly how it will be manifested in each and every circumstance. Even the apostle Paul does not provide specific examples of what submission looks like when he calls wives to submit. This brings us back to the Song of Songs. Essentially, biblical submission requires a wife to

◇◇◇◇◇◇◇◇◇◇◇◇◇◇◇◇◇◇◇◇◇◇◇◇

...submission is *not* something that a husband imposes on his wife, but rather it is a calling which comes to the wife directly from God.

◇◇◇◇◇◇◇◇◇◇◇◇◇◇◇◇◇◇◇◇◇◇◇◇

lean on her husband like the woman does in the Song. By leaning on her husband the woman displays 'an inner quality of gentleness' that affirms her husband's leadership. Submission is not so much an *action* as much as it is an *attitude*.

In addition to the image of the wife leaning on her husband, the Song of Songs provides a second metaphor which helps to capture the essence of the attitude of submission. In Songs chapter 2, the lovers are engaged in a vivid exchange of mutual praise. In the midst of this passionate exchange the woman declares, 'Like an apple tree among the trees of the forest is my lover among the young men. I delight to sit in his shade,' (2:3). Here the woman compares her husband to a tree, declaring that she delights to 'sit in his shade'. Note that the man does not force her to sit in his shade, but rather she delights to sit under his protective leadership and care. Her delight to 'sit in his shade' captures the heart and the essence of the attitude of biblical submission.[15]

The power of submission

Before we leave the topic of submission, I think it would be helpful for wives and prospective wives to contemplate the power of submission. The apostle Peter addresses this issue in his first epistle. He reveals three powerful potential ramifications of submission. First, according to 1 Peter 3:1 a wife's submission may lead to the conversion of her unbelieving husband: 'Wives, in the same way be submissive to your husbands *so that, if any of them do not believe the word, they may be won over without words by the behaviour of their wives,'* (emphasis mine). Second, Peter notes that a wife's submission also enhances her personal beauty: 'For this is the way the holy women of the past who put their hope in God used to make themselves beautiful. *They were submissive to their own husbands,'* (1 Peter 3:5, emphasis mine). Finally, Peter reveals that a wife's submission reflects upon her spiritual maturity. Peter notes that wives who submit to their husbands are daughters of the great matriarch Sarah (1 Peter 3:6). While all of these by-products of submission are wonderful, the real power of wifely submission is that it glorifies Jesus Christ.

Christ: our loving leader

It is not difficult to see how the complementary relationship between husband and wife points us to the love of Christ.

162

All we have to do is read Ephesians 5:22-33! The typology is explicit and truly extraordinary. The Bible tells us that Jesus leads us as a loving husband and we lean upon him as a trusting bride. Therefore, if a husband desires to lead his wife in love he must look to Christ as an example of loving leadership and he must seek Christ for the resurrection power to emulate that loving leadership in his marriage. Likewise, a wife who longs to submit to her husband as a loving response to his leadership must look to Christ's example of submission and must also seek him to empower her to embody the mind of Christ which will allow her to submit in love.

It is important for husbands and wives to recognize that when the New Testament speaks of the leadership of husbands and the submission of wives, both in Ephesians 5 and 1 Peter 3, what precedes these imperatives is the indicative of Christ's work of redemption. The point is that these complementary roles are an outworking of our redemption. They are not a burden of the Fall, but rather they are part of the blessing of the New Covenant. Therefore, husbands and wives should rejoice in these redemptive callings and they should recognize that they will only be in harmony with one another if they look to the example of Christ as their spiritual tuning fork.

It is Jesus Christ who sets an example for all couples by lovingly leading his bride, a bride which trustfully leans upon him for all her needs. Just as the woman in the Song leans upon her husband, spouses who desire to complement one another must lean upon Christ their heavenly bridegroom. When couples do this they will make beautiful music together.

Questions for review and discussion

1. *For everyone*: Read Proverbs 31 and make a list of the variety of activities engaged in by this godly wife. Discuss how these duties challenge and correct gender stereotypes in our culture and in the church.

2. *For couples*: While the Bible does not give us an exact division of labour for husbands and wives, marital harmony is best achieved when couples have agreed upon expectations regarding the division of labour in their marriages. If you are not yet married, discuss with your future spouse how you intend to divide the labour in your home. If you are presently married, discuss the present division of labour in your marriage.

3. *For husbands*: Take the 'Ephesians 5:25 Test' and the 'Ephesians 5:28 Test'. Make a list of times when you have failed to lead your wife in a Christ-like manner. Repent of these sins and ask God to help you to fulfil your calling as a husband. Confess your sins to your wife as well and share with her your desire to lead in accordance with the demands of these verses. If you are not yet married, make a commitment to fulfil the calling of these verses in your marriage.

4. *For wives*: Read 1 Peter 2 and Ephesians 5:1-21. Contemplate how your calling to submit is intimately related to the redemptive work of Christ. Assess yourself to see if you have displayed a biblical attitude of submission in your marriage. Confess to God your failings in these areas and make a commitment to repent of them. Discuss the results of your self-assessment with your husband.

5. *For husbands*: Review John Piper's propositions describing 'mature masculinity'. Assess whether you are displaying

'mature masculinity' when it comes to your relationship with your wife. Discuss this with your wife.

6. **For couples:** Biblical scholar Andreas Köstenberger notes that the Fall involved a reversal of the God-ordained roles of husband and wife. He writes:

> The Fall witnesses a complete reversal of roles assigned by God to the man and the woman. Rather than God being in charge, with the man, helped by the woman, ruling creation for him, a complete reversal takes place: Satan, in the form of a serpent, approaches the woman, who draws the man with her into rebellion against the Creator.[16]

Discuss ways in which our culture replicates this error. Also, examine your own marriage to determine whether this reversal is occurring in your marriage.

9. Maintaining true love:
compliment one another

Sonnet 18

Shall I compare thee to a summer's day?
Thou art more lovely and more temperate...
(William Shakespeare)

♦ ♦ ♦ ♦

'All beautiful you are, my darling; there is no flaw in you,'
(Song of Songs 4:7).

When Adam first laid eyes upon his wife he burst forth in speech. He declared before Eve that she was bone of his bones and flesh of his flesh (Genesis 2:23). In other words, the first thing Adam did in his marriage was to praise his wife. He spoke well of her. He complimented her. It is noteworthy that the first recorded words spoken by a human, and the only words spoken by a human before the Fall, were Adam's assuring words of compliment to his beloved wife. In the previous chapter, we examined how true love is cultivated and maintained when couples *complement* one another. In this chapter, we will see that true love is also enriched and preserved when couples *compliment* one another.

The Song of Songs does not deal with every aspect of communication necessary for a strong marriage.[1] Rather, it focuses primarily on complimentary communication between the lovers. It teaches couples how to speak redemptively. It teaches them how to praise one another, by exploring four categories of complimentary speech. There are compliments of assurance, praise, comparison and satisfaction. Let's look at each of these forms of complimentary speech as they are revealed in the Song of Songs.

Compliments of assurance

Most human beings suffer from a variety of insecurities. This is part of human nature. These insecurities do not disappear after one is married. It is important for spouses to recognize the presence of these insecurities in one another. In destructive marriages, spouses often take these insecurities as opportunities to manipulate and degrade their marriage partner. However, in redemptive marriages, spouses should seek to allay the fears which lie at the core of these insecurities by exchanging compliments of assurance. One of the areas in which spouses most often need reassurance is in regard to their physical appearance. We see an example of this need in the Song of Songs.

In the first chapter of the Song the woman speaks about her longing to be with her lover (1:1-4). Then in Song 1:5 she begins to describe her own perception of her physical appearance, 'Dark am I, yet lovely, O daughters of Jerusalem, dark like the tents of Kedar, like the tent curtains of Solomon.' From this verse one might conclude that the woman is confident about her physical beauty, after all she states that she is dark 'yet lovely'. However, notice how she expresses her insecurity regarding her physical appearance in the very next verse: 'Do not stare at me because I am dark, because I am darkened by the sun. My mother's sons were angry with me and made me take care of the vineyards; my own vineyard I have neglected,' (Song 1:6). Clearly, the woman is uncomfortable with her appearance. Her insecurities regarding her physical appearance lead her to request that her lover not 'stare' at her. Why does she feel so insecure?

She is insecure and embarrassed because of her complexion, the colour of her skin, which has been darkened by the sun. In today's world, we would say that she has a deep sun tan. Why does the woman view her dark skin as unattractive? After all today, in many countries in the West, tanned skin is a prized commodity and a sign of beauty. People even go to sun-tanning salons specifically to acquire the dark skin which the woman in the Song seems to view as so unattractive. However, in the age in which the Song of Songs was written tanned skin was not seen as a thing of beauty, but rather as an inescapable sign that you were engaged in outdoor physical labour. In other words, it meant that you were likely to be lower class and poor. This was the case with the woman in the Song of Songs. In Song 1:6 she notes that she was forced into outdoor labour by her brothers: '...My mother's sons were angry with me *and made me take care of the vineyards...*' (emphasis mine). She goes on to note that this forced labour in the vineyard is directly related to her perceived neglect of her own physical beauty, her own 'vineyard'. She makes this contrast at the end of verse six: '...My mother's sons were angry with me and made me take care of the vineyards; *my own vineyard I have neglected,*' (emphasis mine). How will her lover respond to her insecurity? He responds with a compliment of assurance.

The man responds to his lover's insecurity in a similar way to Adam when he spoke his first words to Eve. As we saw in the introduction to this chapter, the first recorded words of man, the first words of Adam, were a compliment of assurance to his wife: 'This is now bone of my bones and flesh of my flesh,' (Genesis 2:23). Likewise, the first recorded words of the man in the Song of Songs are a compliment of assurance. The man replies to the fears and insecurities she expressed in Song 1:6 by stating in Song 1:8 that she is the 'most beautiful of women'. Do you see the wonderful assurance found in this compliment? He doesn't say to her, 'Yeah, you're a little dark, but I guess you will do.' Nor does he say to her, 'A little cosmetic surgery will fix that.' Rather, he tells this woman feeling the insecurities of her physical appearance that he thinks that she is the 'most beautiful of women'. He gives her a compliment of assurance and he does not stop at verse eight.

In Song 1:9-11 the man expands his compliment of assurance by continuing to speak of the woman's physical beauty: 'I liken you, my darling, to a mare harnessed to one of the chariots of Pharaoh. Your cheeks are beautiful with earrings, your neck with strings of jewels. We will make you earrings of gold, studded with silver.' In these verses, by means of poetic metaphor, the man assures the woman of her physical beauty. While it is quite easy to grasp the comparisons of her cheeks and neck with the stunning beauty of jewellery, there is one metaphor in this verse which is difficult to understand at first glance. He begins the verse by comparing the woman to a 'mare harnessed to one of the chariots of Pharaoh'. Now at first this will strike the modern reader as a rather odd way to compliment a woman! After all, in our day comparing a woman to a horse is anything but flattering! However, what lies underneath this metaphor is a powerful statement of the woman's beauty.

In the ancient Near East, particularly in Egypt, war was conducted with the use of chariots which were led by stallions (male horses). One of the defence tactics used to counter the attack of chariots was to set a mare (a female horse) on heat loose on the battlefield. The purpose of this tactic was to send the stallions into mass confusion by distracting them with a mare ready to mate.[2] Therefore, what the man is saying by comparing the woman to a mare is that her physical beauty is so profound that it is distracting him much like the stallions on the battlefield. What a grand compliment indeed!

In this opening exchange of the Song, we witness the man allaying the fears and insecurities of his love by speaking a compliment of assurance. She is filled with a sense of physical unattractiveness and the man replies by calling her the 'most beautiful of women' and one who is so gorgeous that her beauty drives him to distraction. Later in the Song of Songs the man assures his lover again of her physical beauty by issuing the following compliment: 'All beautiful you are, my darling;

there is no flaw in you,' (Song 4:7).[3] The man responds to his lover's insecurities with compliments of assurance.

Like the woman in the Song of Songs, almost every human being feels physically inadequate and unattractive at times. Insecurity with regard to physical appearance has only been heightened in our age by the proliferation of images through mass media. We now have these ideal, unattainable and unreal standards of beauty set before our eyes every day. Men encounter images of the hulky athletic type with burgeoning biceps and a washboard stomach. Women encounter images of the supermodel with long shapely legs and a tiny waist. It's no wonder that so many people feel inadequate and insecure regarding their physical appearance. A loving spouse will recognize this insecurity in his or her mate and, like the man in the Song of Songs, will purposefully convey compliments of assurance to quell them. Couples must never forget the need to continue to assure one another in this area.

Compliments of pure praise

While compliments of assurance are necessary to maintain the vitality of true love, the Song of Songs reveals that the purpose of complimentary communication extends beyond mere assurance. In the Song of Songs, the lovers also exchange compliments of pure praise.

At first the phrase 'compliments of pure praise' may sound redundant. After all, every compliment, by definition, must contain some level of praise. However, the point I am trying to make by employing this phrase is that while some categories of compliments have a specific purpose (i.e. to assure), there is a category of compliment which is given for no pragmatic purpose at all. This type of compliment is pure praise. It is praise for praise's sake. It is given because lovers enjoy extolling their partners. While the Song of Songs contains many examples of this category of compliment, we'll focus on just one representative example which is found in Song 1:15 - 2:3.

In this section of the Song the two lovers go back and forth issuing vivid and rich compliments of praise in three couplets. One commentator appropriately refers to this section of the Song as 'a duet of mutual admiration'.[4] There is no purpose given for this praise. The lovers just seem to enjoy praising one another. Let us focus on the substance of the first of these praise couplets (Song 1:15-16) to get a sense of how these lovers revel in praising one another:

Man: 'How beautiful you are, my darling! Oh, how beautiful! Your eyes are doves,' (v. 15).

Woman: 'How handsome you are, my lover! Oh, how charming! And our bed is verdant,' (v. 16).

The man begins this couplet of praise by declaring that his lover is beautiful. In fact, he declares her beauty twice in this verse for emphasis. He also uses a term of endearment by referring to her as his 'darling'. The praise informs the woman that she has both the man's physical and emotional affection. He then closes his praise by referring to her eyes. He declares to her, 'Your eyes are doves.' What does this metaphor imply?

173

There are many suggestions. Some commentators contend that the man is praising the shape of the woman's eyes — they are oval like a dove. Others suggest that the metaphor refers to the innocence and timidity of her eyes — they flutter like the wings of a dove. Although it is difficult to determine the exact meaning of this metaphor, what is clear is that the man is praising the beauty of his lover's eyes and he is doing it while gazing deeply into the depths of them.

The woman responds to the man's praise with her own salvo of praise. Her response meets his praise point for point. The man extolled her beauty twice and now the woman responds in like manner by declaring that he is both 'handsome' and 'charming'. The man used the term of endearment 'darling' and now the woman responds with the term of 'lover'. She closes her praise by referring to the fruitful joy of their love: 'And our bed is verdant.' In other words, their love flourishes and blooms like a healthy tree.

It is important for couples to realize the value of this type of praise. The lovers' exchange of praise is not superficial flattery. Their words do not compare to the shallow romantic babblings which are found in cheap romance novels and pastel greeting cards. Rather, their praise wells up from their deep reservoir of love. Their words of praise have been carefully contemplated and were forged in the foundry of their hearts.

This isn't cheap praise. It isn't pragmatic praise which is manipulative or which seeks its own benefit. This is pure praise. It is complimentary praise which enriches the love shared by the couple.

Compliments of comparison

The couple in the Song also engage in a third category of complimentary language — compliments of comparison. This form of complimentary language is used by the lovers to convey to one another that they have no competitors. In effect, the lovers use compliments of comparison as a means of setting one another apart from all other potential suitors. While the Song of Songs contains numerous examples of this form of compliment, again we'll look at just one representative example, found in Song of Songs 2:2-3:

> *Man:* 'Like a lily among thorns is my darling among the maidens,' (v. 2).

> *Woman:* 'Like an apple tree among the trees of the forest is my lover among the young men,' (v. 3).

The man commences this exchange by comparing the woman to all the eligible women he could choose to love — 'the maidens'. He sets his lover apart from these potential competitors by declaring that she is 'like a lily among thorns'. By this metaphor the man declares that all the other 'maidens' are like thorns, while his lover is like a lily among them. The choice is clear. His lover stands out. She rises head and shoulders above the rest. Through this compliment of comparison the man tells his lover that she has no rival.

The woman responds to the man's compliment in symmetrical fashion. She compares her lover to all the eligible men she could choose to love — 'the young men'. She too uses

> We must tell our spouses that they are not in competition for our love. We must let them know that they are set apart in our hearts.

a metaphor to set him apart from the competition: 'like an apple tree among the trees of the forest'. This metaphor declares to her lover that he beats all the competitors. He is like an apple tree which provides beautiful fragrant blossoms and rich nourishing fruit. In comparison, the other young men are like boring, uniform and common trees. There is nothing outstanding about them. They are a bland forest. Again the choice is clear. By her compliment of comparison she communicates to him that he has no rival.

Compliments of comparison are extremely important to a healthy and secure romantic relationship. We must tell our spouses that they are not in competition for our love. We must let them know that they are set apart in our hearts. We must let our spouses know, by compliments of comparison, that we have set our affections exclusively on them. We must tell them that we have forsaken all others.

Compliments of satisfaction

The final form of complimentary language found in the Song is what I refer to as compliments of satisfaction. This form of complimentary language is used by the lovers to convey to each other that they have found complete romantic fulfilment in one another. This form of compliment is used to confirm to one another that they find nothing lacking in their romantic relationship which would lead them to search elsewhere. Once again, there are many examples of this form of complimentary language in the Song, but we will look at just one in order to capture the essence of the nature of this form of compliment.

In Song of Songs 4:10-11 the man informs his lover that he finds complete fulfilment in her love by declaring:

> How delightful is your love, my sister, my bride! How much more pleasing is your love than wine, and the fragrance of your perfume than any spice! Your lips drop sweetness as the honeycomb, my bride; milk and honey are under your tongue. The fragrance of your garments is like that of Lebanon
>
> (Song 4:10-11).

In these verses the man declares to the woman that her love is 'delightful' and that it is more pleasing 'than wine'. He also states that her perfume is more pleasing 'than any spice'. He continues to build on his expression of satisfaction by stating that her lips 'drop sweetness as the honeycomb' and that 'milk and honey' are under her tongue. Here he conveys that her kisses are sweet, pleasant, rich and satisfying. The combination of milk and honey points to abundance and full satisfaction. This is seen elsewhere in Scripture when the metaphor of milk and honey is used to describe the rich abundance of the land of Israel — the Promised Land (Exodus 3:8). Finally, the man states that the fragrance of her clothes is 'like that of Lebanon'. This is most likely a reference to the fresh and welcoming fragrance of the cedars of Lebanon. By these phrases he is informing his bride that all of his physical longings find their satisfaction in her and in her alone. She satisfies a variety of his senses — taste, touch and smell. The man makes certain that his lover knows that she fully satisfies his wants and desires.

The Bible calls us to find complete physical satisfaction in our spouses and in them alone. Proverbs 5:18-20 expresses this biblical command concisely:

> May your fountain be blessed, and may you rejoice in the wife of your youth. A loving doe, a graceful deer — may her breasts satisfy you always, may you ever be captivated by her love. Why be captivated, my son, by an adulteress? Why embrace the bosom of another man's wife?

Compliments of satisfaction express the heart of this biblical principle. They remind our spouses that they are the *only* one through whom we satisfy our physical desires. These types of compliments not only encourage our spouses, but they also inform them that our eyes and hearts are not roaming elsewhere for satisfaction. Compliments of satisfaction communicate to our spouses that we are satisfied and captivated with them and them alone.

Cultivating a complimentary relationship

The Song of Songs teaches us that true love must be expressed verbally as well as physically. A healthy romance must include complimentary language. We must communicate to our spouse compliments of assurance, pure praise, comparison and satisfaction. Ultimately, all of these complimentary forms of speech converge to convey to our spouses that they are the love of our lives. One of the warning signs of the onset of marital decay is when our mouths cease to speak compliments to our spouses. Given the importance of complimentary speech, let me give you some suggestions which will help you cultivate a complimentary relationship with your spouse.

> Compliments of satisfaction communicate to our spouses that we are satisfied and captivated with them and them alone.

First, you must engage in self-assessment. You must evaluate whether you are by nature a person who compliments well. Frankly, people are different when it comes to their effectiveness in complimenting others. Some people are able to share compliments with ease and will have no problem with this type of communication. However, other people are less willing in this area and share compliments only begrudgingly. Therefore, you must begin by assessing yourself. If you come to the conclusion that you are not naturally oriented to this type of speech this does not get you off the hook! Rather, this means that you must work hard at improving this area of your marriage. You will need to be more purposeful and deliberate in your complimenting. You will have to develop a vocabulary of praise. A helpful place to start is by acquainting yourself with romantic literature like the Song of Songs and other forms of human love poetry. Don't attempt to force it, but wait until your compliments become genuine and sincere.

Second, take some time to think about your spouse. Our lives are so busy and it is easy to take for granted their special and unique attributes. Set apart some time to contemplate the virtues of your spouse. Study your spouse. Ask yourself the following questions: What are my spouse's insecurities? Why do I find my spouse physically attractive? What sets my spouse apart from all others? How does my spouse please and satisfy me?

Third, recognize that compliments need not be restricted to the area of physical beauty and romance. We should praise our spouses for all the things they do well. For example, Proverbs 31 notes that a husband should praise his wife for her work. In fact, this text suggests that the noble work of a wife is to be esteemed more highly than the fleeting attributes of charm and beauty:

> Her children arise and call her blessed; *her husband also, and he praises her*: 'Many women do noble things, but you surpass them all.' Charm is deceptive, and beauty is fleeting; but a woman who fears the LORD is to be praised. Give her the reward she has earned, and let her works bring her praise at the city gate
>
> (Proverbs 31:28-31, emphasis mine).

Obviously, a wife should also follow a similar pattern in complimenting her husband. She should praise him for his work as a father and husband. She should also praise him for his work outside the home. She should praise him for all those things he does well.

Finally, learn to find joy in complimenting your spouse. Be like the lovers in the Song. Revel in the joy of crafting unique compliments in the workshop of your heart. Complimenting the love of our life is meant to be enjoyable both for the giver and the recipient of the compliment. Complimenting our spouses should be a labour of love.

The healing power of words

The point of this chapter is that couples should not underestimate the impact that words can have on the health of their marriage. Words can destroy or they can heal. They can kill or they can bring life. They can degrade or they can edify. The Song calls on lovers to use words that will heal, bring life and edify. In fact, the Song *demands* it. We are to use the power of words to adorn our spouses, not tear them down. In their book *Intimate Allies* Tremper Longman and Dan Allender note that God made and shaped this world by his spoken word. By the word of his mouth he brought life and order out of chaos and emptiness. Allender and Longman suggest that husbands and wives are to follow a similar pattern regarding the use of words in the marital relationship: 'God also calls husbands and wives to use our words to push back the chaos and shape our lives into order and beauty. He calls us to use our words to bring life to those who hear them.'[5] Begin the process of bringing order and beauty to your marriage by complimenting your spouse; begin, as Marva Dawn suggests, to recognize the redemptive power of 'saying love' in your marriage. She notes that 'saying love' always conveys to our spouse our covenant faithfulness to them:

181

Whether the love-saying is wild and passionate or gentle and consoling, whether it is laughing and crazy or serious and divulging, it always speaks faithfulness. Each time we say love it is a covenant, a spiritual act. It is a reminder that we have promised to be faithful, that we are knit together in this special bond of oneness for the purposes of God.[6]

By complimenting one another spouses can fortify the bonds of their oneness. They can come closer to realizing the essence of the first compliment spoken by one spouse to another, 'This is now bone of my bones and flesh of my flesh,' (Genesis 2:23).

The one who speaks well of us

The biblical pattern of spouses complimenting one another, like many other aspects of human love, finds a parallel in the divine-human relationship. The Old Testament reveals that God was Israel's husband. The New Testament teaches us that it is specifically Christ who serves as the bridegroom of the New Covenant church. Jesus is our divine husband and we, the church, are his bride. The Bible reveals that our divine husband speaks to us in ways that edify us.

First, God edifies us by speaking his law to us. The words of God's law are not harsh and they are not to be considered as an onerous burden to the believer. Rather, they are intended to be received by us as words of sweetness and love. Psalm 19 reflects how the believer should view God's laws: 'They are more precious than gold, than much pure gold; they are sweeter than honey, than honey from the comb. By them is your servant warned; in keeping them there is great reward,' (Psalm 19:10-11). Just as the man in the Song found sweetness in the mouth of his lover, a believer should find sweetness in the words spoken from the mouth of God. As Matthew Henry notes, 'In the word of God there is sweet and wholesome nourishment, milk for babes, honey for those that are grown up.'[7] God's law is a form of speech by which he edifies and builds up his spouse. Through his law he adorns his spouse and sets her apart from all others.

However, God does not only speak words of edification to his bride; he also compliments her. Much like the lovers in the Song, God speaks well of his spouse. Most of us probably have not considered the joy Christ takes in us as his bride. Roger Ellsworth puts it this way: 'But how many of us think of Christ and his love for his church in these terms? How many of us think of him as being smitten with the beauty of the church? How many of us think of Christ as exclaiming, "How fair!" when he speaks of his heavenly bride.'[8] Ellsworth notes that the Bible frequently speaks of God taking joy in us and speaking well of us and cites the following Old Testament texts to prove his point:[9]

- 'For the LORD *takes delight* in his people; he crowns the humble with salvation,' (Psalm 149:4, emphasis mine).
- 'As a young man marries a maiden, so will your sons marry you; *as a bridegroom rejoices over his bride, so will your God rejoice over you*,' (Isaiah 62:5, emphasis mine).
- 'The LORD your God is with you, he is mighty to save. *He will take great delight in you, he will quiet you with his love,*

he will rejoice over you with singing,' (Zephaniah 3:17, emphasis mine).

Remember, the church finds herself in a very similar position to the woman in the Song. The church, as a bride, is concerned with her lack of perfection and beauty, but her husband speaks compliments of assurance to her. Jesus refers to his bride as the 'flawless one'. Although we are a sinful bride, Christ makes us flawless. In Ephesians 5:26-27 the apostle Paul informs us that Jesus will cleanse us with his word, make us radiant, remove all our stains and wrinkles. Jesus promises to make us a pure and beautiful virgin, a bride that is 'holy and blameless'. One day the bride will stand before her heavenly bridegroom, wrapped in the robes of his righteousness, and Jesus will declare her utterly flawless; he will state that she is the most beautiful of women. That will be the greatest compliment of all!

Knowing that your heavenly husband edifies and speaks well of you, follow his example by doing the same with your earthly spouse. Maintain the vitality of your marital love by complimenting one another.

Questions for review and discussion

1. *In Ephesians 4:29 the apostle Paul issues the following command to Christians: 'Do not let any unwholesome talk come out of your mouths, but only what is helpful for building others up according to their needs, that it may benefit those who listen.' Jay Adams rightly notes that when Paul refers to 'unwholesome talk' in this verse he is not just calling Christians to avoid using*

184

'foul language', but rather he is calling on them to avoid using 'words — God's great gift for communication — to cut up one another'.[10] Consider how you are using words in your marriage. Are you building up your spouse according to his or her needs or are you tearing your spouse down? Discuss this issue with your spouse to gain his or her assessment regarding how well you are communicating.

2. In this chapter we looked at four different types of compliments: compliments of assurance, pure praise, comparison and satisfaction. Complete the chart below with an example of each of these forms of compliments which you can then share with your spouse this week:

Form of compliment	*Compliment*
Compliment of assurance	_____
Compliment of pure praise	_____
Compliment of comparison	_____
Compliment of satisfaction	_____

3. Read the following sections from the Song of Songs and attempt to classify the forms of compliments found in them: 4:1-7; 5:10-16; 6:4-10; 6:13 - 7:9; 7:7-9. Also, consider how you might use these passages to guide your own efforts to compliment your spouse.

4. Read the following texts and meditate on the love of Jesus Christ which manifests itself in the fact that he declares, and makes you, flawless: Ephesians 5:22-32; 2 Corinthians 5:21; 1 John 3:1-2; Jude 1:24-25; and Revelation 21:2.

10. Maintaining true love:
a glorious reunion

*Christians are not to pattern their lives after the cultural
patterns of this world. Their love-making may not follow
the pattern set by Hollywood ... God, the Lord, who has
committed all authority to the Son, through whom he rules all
things, has given direction for our love life...*

(Henry Van Til)

♦ ♦ ♦ ♦

*'Awake, north wind, and come, south wind! Blow on my garden,
that its fragrance may spread abroad. Let my lover come into his
garden and taste its choice fruits. I have come into my garden, my
sister, my bride; I have gathered my myrrh with my spice. I have
eaten my honeycomb and my honey; I have drunk my wine and
my milk. Eat, O friends, and drink; drink your fill, O lovers,'*

(Song of Songs 4:16 - 5:1).

God made humans sexual creatures. One could properly say that humans were created for sex; that is, God designed us for sex and, in fact, commanded us to engage in the activity in the context of the marital relationship. Sex is central both to human nature and to God's plan for this world. Consider, for example, what God declared when he created humanity:

> Then God said, 'Let us make *man in our image, in our likeness*, and let them rule over the fish of the sea and the birds of the air, over the livestock, over all the earth, and over all the creatures that move along the ground.' *So God created man in his own image, in the image of God he created him; male and female he created them.* God blessed them and said to them, *'Be fruitful and increase* in number; fill the earth and subdue it. Rule over the fish of the sea and the birds of the air and over every living creature that moves on the ground,'
>
> (Genesis 1:26-28, emphasis mine).

From these verses we learn that the existence of human sexuality ('male and female he created them') is directly related to humanity being made in the image of God ('So God created man in his own image, in the image of God he created him'). Furthermore, these verses teach us that sexual reproduction is central to God's plan for humanity and this world (God blessed them and said to them, 'Be fruitful and increase in number; fill the earth and subdue it'). Sex is part of who we are and what we are called to do in God's world. In fact, God not only commands sex, but he blesses it as well. It is important to recognize that this revelation regarding human sexuality occurs in the pre-Fall period. What this tells us is that even in a world without sin God commanded sex. Therefore, sex is not something that is sinful or dirty. God created us to be sexual beings and we can glorify him when we engage in this blessed activity with our spouse.

Given that God created husbands and wives for sex, commanded them to have sex, and pronounced a blessing upon their sexual activity, we can safely assume that this is an important part of married life. When spouses unite sexually they are doing something profound because human sexuality unites male and female in a unique way. In fact, as John Stott notes, sex is 'more than a union; it is a kind of *reunion* ... it is the union of two persons who originally were one, were then separated from each other, and now in the sexual encounter of marriage come together again' (emphasis mine).[1] According to the Bible, human sexuality is a glorious reunion!

The Song of Songs reminds us of this wonderful truth. Of all the books in the Bible, it is the Song which most specifically strives to fathom the depths of the glorious reunion of husband and wife. The Song explores the mystery of human sexuality through the power and passion of poetry. It provides us with a biblical view of sex. In fact, it provides us with a puritanical view of sex. Let me explain.

A puritanical view of sex

The world often charges Christians with being 'puritanical' when it comes to the matter of sex. Oh, if only that were true! Of course, our culture uses the word 'puritanical' as a pejorative term. In our culture to label one as 'puritanical' means that they are prudish, repressed and inhibited when it comes to sex. In reality, the Puritans were anything but prudish, repressed and inhibited in this matter. In fact, they were instrumental in unleashing sex from the chains of medieval theology.

Medieval theology considered sexuality as a necessary evil at best. According to many early church and medieval theologians, procreation was the only purpose for sex and even that purpose was not to be celebrated. For example, Augustine (354-430) often commended married couples who abstained from sexual relations; Jerome (347-420) believed that the only good that came from sexual activity was that it produced virgins; and Ambrose (340-397) thought that married people ought to blush over the state in which they lived.[2] In fact, the Council of Trent, the Roman Catholic response to the Reformation, denounced anyone who maintained that virginity was not superior to marriage.[3] The Reformers, and the Puritans who followed them, had a very different view of human sexuality.

Leland Ryken has done a wonderful study of the Puritan view of sex in his book entitled *Worldly Saints: The Puritans As They Really Were.*[4] According to Ryken, the Puritans believed the following regarding sex:

1. *Sex is a 'God-implanted natural or biological appetite'.* For the Puritans, to desire sex was as natural as desiring food or drink. Sex is a good desire and satisfying it should be a joyful and pleasurable experience.

2. *Sex is more than a mere physical act.* For the Puritans, sex was 'part of a total union of two persons, including their minds, emotions, and souls as well as their bodies'.
3. *Sex is an absolute necessity in marriage.* The Puritans were insistent that married couples must engage in sex on a regular basis in order to satisfy their godly appetites and avoid the sin of adultery.
4. *Sex is an honourable and private matter between spouses.* While the Puritans were quite liberated in their view of sexual enjoyment, they had an 'abhorrence of erotic displays in public, where the sexual urges of others might be inflamed'.[5]

As you can see, the Puritans were no prudes when it came to sex. In fact, the great Puritan William Gouge declared that married people should engage in sexual relations 'with good will and delight, willingly, readily, and cheerfully'.[6] Modern Christians should follow the pattern and principles of the Puritans when it comes to sex. Christians should be puritanical! These Puritan principles of sexuality are all revealed in the Song of Songs. Let's look at each one these principles as they emerge in the Song, particularly in Song of Songs 4:16 - 5:1.

Sex is a natural desire which is pleasurable to satisfy

G. K. Chesterton once insightfully quipped, 'Every man who knocks on the door of a brothel is looking for God.' The point Chesterton was making is that the desire for sex is a God-given desire and even when it is misdirected it still speaks of who

191

God created us to be. The Puritans understood that sexual desire is a gift of God and that the satisfying of this desire in marriage should be as natural and pleasurable as the satisfying of our daily needs for food and drink. Eating and drinking are natural functions and while humans could live on a bland diet of bread and water, God has chosen to give us rich, tasty and wonderful foods to nourish us. The Scriptures are replete with references to the pleasing aroma and taste of rich and hearty foods. Satisfying our natural appetite for food is both functional *and* enjoyable. In like manner, God created humans with an appetite for sex and he made sex both functional (it is necessary to propagate the race) and pleasurable. We see this principle in the Song of Songs.

Interestingly, the lovers in the Song compare the pleasure of the consummation of their sexual relationship to that of the pleasure of eating satisfying foods. For example, in Song 5:1 the husband expresses the sexual satisfaction and joy he has experienced in his encounter with his wife by stating, 'I have eaten my honeycomb and my honey; I have drunk my wine and my milk.' The husband compares their sexual union in terms of a delightful feast. Honey, wine and milk are all sweet and satisfying foods and the husband has had his fill — he has 'eaten' and he has 'drunk'.

The duplication present in the husband's words also suggest the superlative nature of the fulfilment he has found in his wife. He has not only eaten honeycomb, but also honey. He has not only tasted wine, but also milk. He is fully satisfied with his wife. The husband's experience is in accord with the words of Proverbs 5:18-19: 'May your fountain be blessed, and may you rejoice in the wife of your youth. A loving doe, a graceful deer — may her breasts satisfy you always, may you ever be captivated by her love.' The husband in the Song is both captivated and satisfied.

This theme of pleasurable satisfaction is echoed by the comments which follow the husband's declaration in Song 5:1: 'Eat, O friends, and drink; drink your fill, O lovers.' While there is some debate regarding exactly who is speaking here, the meaning of the imperative is clear.[7] As Tom Gledhill puts it, 'There is to be no reserve, no restraint, but a complete and happy enjoyment of each other in their mutual love.'[8] The lovers are to have their fill. They are to satisfy their sexual appetites.

The Song of Songs teaches Christians that sex is meant to be pleasurable and satisfying. As long as sex occurs within the bounds of marriage, it is neither wrong to desire it nor to take pleasure in it. This principle is reiterated in the New Testament where we frequently find the apostle Paul battling those who attempt to deny the satisfying of God-given desires such as the joy of eating certain foods and the joy of sex. For example, in 1 Timothy the apostle condemns a certain class of false teachers specifically because, 'They forbid people to marry and order them to abstain from certain foods, which God created to be received with thanksgiving by those who believe and who know the truth,' (1 Timothy 4:3). Paul attacks this type of asceticism with incredible ferocity because it is

> As long as sex occurs within the bounds of marriage, it is neither wrong to desire it nor to take pleasure in it.

inherently unbiblical. Paul states the biblical principle regarding these matters in the verses which follow his condemnation of these false teachers: 'For everything God created is good, and nothing is to be rejected if it is received with thanksgiving, because it is consecrated by the word of God and prayer,' (1 Timothy 4:4-5).

As Christians live together as husband and wife they must make certain that they have a redeemed view of human sexuality. Sex is not dirty and to desire it is not wrong. Sexual desire only becomes wrong when it is misplaced or when it exceeds the parameters of God's word. Therefore, it is important for couples to be open and honest with each other about their sexual desires so that these natural appetites can be satisfied within the confines of the marital relationship and thereby keeping the marriage bed 'undefiled' (Hebrew 13:4, NKJV). While there is never an excuse for sexual sins such as prostitution, pornography, masturbation and adultery, couples must realize that these sins are more likely to occur in relationships in which couples do not seek to satisfy one another's natural sexual desires. Paul makes this very point in 1 Corinthians 7:5 where he warns couples that if they refrain from sexual activity for extended periods of time they run the risk of being tempted by Satan and losing their self-control.

The Bible teaches that sexual desires are natural and satisfying them is enjoyable. Do you have a biblical mindset regarding sexual desire? Are you protecting your marriage by fulfilling the sexual desires of your spouse? If not, transform your mind and your marriage by reorienting your sex life according to God's word.

Sex is more than a physical act

While the Song of Songs certainly celebrates the physical pleasure of sex, it does not limit sex to a mere physical act. In addition, while the desire for sex is a natural appetite akin to our appetite for food, that does not mean that we should *fully* equate the two appetites. As Tom Gledhill properly notes, 'But the "one flesh" union is meant to be more than a physical act like eating. Behind the physical there is the relational, the interaction at a psychological, personal level.'[9] Although sex is a natural appetite, it must never be reduced to a mere biological function. Sex involves the totality of the lives of two people. We see this principle in the Song of Songs.

The sexual encounter between the husband and wife in the Song does not occur in a relationship vacuum, rather it occurs in the context of a deeply cultivated, multi-faceted and totally committed relationship. The deep relationship which exists between the couple in the Song is revealed in the substance of the dialogue which precedes the consummation of their physical relationship. In Song of Songs 4:9-15, the section immediately preceding the main sexual encounter of the Song, the husband speaks to his wife regarding his undying and unfailing commitment to her. This sentiment particularly emerges in Song 4:9 where the husband declares to his wife, 'You have stolen my heart, my sister, my bride; you have stolen my heart with one glance of your eyes, with one jewel of your necklace.' This declaration reveals that the husband's heart was given to his wife long before he gave himself physically to her. He was enchanted by her eyes long before he encountered her body. She had his heart before she had his body. She was his sister before she was his bride. The sex experienced by the lovers in the Song occurs at the end of a long process of emotional and romantic bonding.

It is interesting to note that this main sexual encounter between the lovers commences in Song 4:16 with the woman using the word 'awake': '*Awake*, north wind, and come, south wind! Blow on my garden, that its fragrance may spread abroad. Let my lover come into his garden and taste its choice fruits,' (emphasis mine). The use of the word 'awake' in this section is intriguing because this is the very same word that she employed in Song 2:7 to suppress the inappropriate awakening of sexual desire: 'Daughters of Jerusalem, I charge you by the gazelles and by the does of the field: Do not arouse or *awaken* love until it so desires,' (emphasis mine).[10] What has changed since Song 2:7? Now she is married. Now she finds herself in a relationship of trust, love and commitment. Now it is appropriate for her to awaken her desire and enjoy it in its fulness. She is experiencing sex in the context of a covenantal relationship. As Marva Dawn notes, 'Sexual intercourse is such a profound sharing of ourselves with our partner that it needs to be protected — within the covenant of a lifelong, faithful commitment. When God's design is followed, how freeing it is for all the persons involved!'[11] Sex is more than a physical act.

Our culture attempts to contradict this biblical teaching. Our culture attempts to treat sex as if it were *only* a physical act. Our culture treats sex as a physical performance, almost like it is a sport. The pharmaceutical industry even produces performance-enhancing drugs for the sport of sex. The Song of Songs gives an entirely different view. It teaches that meaningful and satisfying sex cannot occur in a vacuum. According to the Song, sex is not a simple act of human biology, but rather a complex encounter which encompasses all that we are. The Song tells us that sex should only occur at the right moment and in the right context. For the lovers in the Song sex should only occur when all has been ordered according to God's design.

The Song of Song calls on married couples to create a context for sex, rather than treating it as a mere physical act. What is your view of sex? Are you, like the surrounding culture, treating sex as *only* a physical appetite or *merely* a biological function? Are you cultivating a context which enhances the meaning of your glorious reunion with your spouse? Are you building the spiritual, psychological and emotional foundations necessary to experience the fulness of redeemed human sexuality?

Sex is an absolute necessity in marriage

The third principle expressed by the Puritans and the Song of Songs is that sex is an essential component of married life. It is no mere coincidence that the structural centrepiece, or climax, of the Song of Songs is the sexual union of the couple. This union was placed in the exact middle of the book because it serves as the evidence, the distinguishing mark, that the couple are married.[12] While this is a bit of an overstatement, it is fair to say that marriage and sex go hand in hand. Although it is important to point out that there are some legitimate circumstances which make it impossible for married people to engage in sexual relations, the overwhelming norm of God's Word is that married people should do so on a regular basis.

This is an indication of a healthy marriage. The apostle Paul alludes to this principle in 1 Corinthians 7 where he prohibits husbands and wives from refraining from sexual activity for extended periods:

> The husband should fulfil his marital duty to his wife, and likewise the wife to her husband. The wife's body does not belong to her alone but also to her husband. In the same way, the husband's body does not belong to him alone but also to his wife. Do not deprive each other except by mutual consent and for a time, so that you may devote yourselves to prayer. Then come together again so that Satan will not tempt you because of your lack of self-control
>
> (1 Corinthians 7:3-5).

In this text, Paul speaks of sex as an essential component of married life. He refers to it as a marital 'duty' which exists because spouses have mutual ownership of one another's bodies. Paul is not insinuating that sex should be a chore. His point is that sex is so central a part of the fabric of marriage that to cease engaging in it places the entire marriage in jeopardy. New Testament scholar Robert Gromacki summarizes Paul's point as follows: 'Marriage without sex is not only unnatural, but it is expressly forbidden.'[13] The Puritans took this biblical principle so seriously that there are records of excommunications based on the refusal of a spouse to engage in sexual relations.[14]

Like 1 Corinthians 7, the Song of Songs teaches the principle of mutual ownership between husband and wife. This principle is revealed in Song 4:16 where the woman declares, 'Awake, north wind, and come, south wind! Blow on my garden, that its fragrance may spread abroad. Let my lover come into his garden and taste its choice fruits.' In this verse the woman refers to their sexual love by means of the metaphor of a 'garden'. What is noteworthy is that in verse 16 she refers to this garden as both 'my garden' and 'his garden'. The point is exactly the same as in 1 Corinthians 7:4: 'The wife's body does not belong to her alone but also to her husband. In the same way, the husband's body does not belong to him alone but also to his wife.' The woman is acknowledging that her body, and her sexuality, no longer belong to her alone, but they also belong to her husband. Of course, the principle applies to the man as well. His body, and his sexuality, now belong to her as well.

God's command for man and woman to become 'one flesh' suggests that sex is an integral part of marriage (Genesis 2:24). Sex is not only enjoyable, but it is absolutely necessary for a healthy marriage. Spouses who deny their partners sex, or use it as a tool of manipulation, are putting their entire marriage at risk by acting contrary to God's command. Are you committing this sin? Has sex become a tool of manipulation in your marriage? Do you understand that your body is no longer entirely your own? Do you recognize that God calls you to freely and voluntarily share yourself sexually with your spouse?

Sex is an honourable and private matter

In this chapter, we have been examining the important role which sex plays in the marital relationship. We have seen that sex is both natural and necessary in a marriage. However, while sex does play a prominent role in marriage, that does not mean it should play a public role. The Bible calls couples to treat their sexuality as a private matter. This means we are to treat sex with honour and dignity. Again, our culture does not understand this biblical principle. In our culture, sexuality is celebrated publicly. It is also treated as a subject for crude humour. This publicizing of human sexuality takes something which is precious and beautiful and renders it an offence. As one social commentator put it, 'Sex is like sand on the beach — one thing when it's lying around sparkling in the sun, quite another when it's kicked in your face.'[15] According to the Bible, couples must treat sex as an honourable and private matter.

The Song of Songs, a book which clearly celebrates the goodness of sex, also treats sex in a dignified and honourable way. For example, the Song is never crude or blunt when it discusses sexuality, but rather it employs subtle and carefully crafted metaphors to describe sexual activity. The Song is never ostentatious when it comes to sexuality. It speaks with a soft and indirect voice.

The Song also displays that the couple treated their sexuality as a private matter. This principle of privacy is most starkly revealed in the Song through the metaphor of the garden. The woman uses the garden as a metaphor for her sexuality. She keeps this garden locked. She keeps it only for her husband. She keeps it private. For example, as the lovers approach the consummation of their relationship the man refers to his wife as follows: 'You are a *garden locked up*, my sister, my bride; you are a spring enclosed, a sealed fountain,' (Song 4:12, emphasis mine). However, when they reach the sexual consummation the woman invites the man to enter her garden, 'Let my lover come into his garden and taste its choice fruits,' (Song of Songs 4:16, emphasis mine). Only one person, her husband, has access to her sexuality. As Tremper Longman notes, 'her heretofore private garden will now become public, at least to the man'.[16]

The couple's desire for privacy permeates the entire Song. One of the constant yearnings of the couple in the Song is to withdraw from the public and enjoy the fulness of their marriage in intimate privacy. This longing for privacy emerges in the final verse of the Song where the woman declares, 'Come away, my lover, and be like a gazelle or like a young stag on the spice-laden mountains,' (Song of Songs 8:14, emphasis mine).

Sex is an honourable and private matter. Are you treating your sexual relationship with your spouse in accord with this principle? This relationship with your spouse is not a matter for discussions over coffee breaks at work, nor is it a matter for joking. Remember the words of Archbishop William Temple, 'The reason for not joking about sex is exactly the same as for not joking about the Holy Communion. It is not that the subject is nasty, but that it is sacred, and to joke about it is profanity.' Make certain that you are treating your glorious reunion with your spouse with the sacred honour and privacy it deserves.

> Make certain that you are treating your glorious reunion with your spouse with the sacred honour and privacy it deserves.

Experiencing the glorious reunion

The lovers in the Song of Songs experience a glorious reunion. They experience a full-orbed love which encompasses all their senses and every part of their being. They experience the fulness of joy which God has given to humanity through the gift of sexuality. It is important to realize that the fulness of this love is something which can be experienced by every Christian couple. In fact, Christians should experience the joys of sexuality at a much greater level than the world because Christians know both the designer and purpose of sex. In other words, Christians have the instruction manual to human sexuality. Marva Dawn illustrates this point by comparing sex to an old typewriter that she used before computers were prevalent. She recalls that when her old typewriter malfunctioned she was able to quickly remedy the problem by referring to the instruction manual. She concludes:

> Why could that instruction book solve my problem every time? It is because the company that built the typewriter wrote the instruction book. Those who know the design of the machine are the ones most able to teach me how the machine can be most effectively used and maintained. That is how our sexuality is like my typewriter.[17]

Dawn's point is that God is our designer. He made us and knows us intimately. He also revealed to us how we are to function sexually in the Bible. In other words, the designer of the human machine has left us with an instruction manual to our sexuality. The Song of Songs is a significant part of that instruction manual. Therefore, because Christians have the designer's instruction manual they should be able to experience sex which is healthy, joyful and pleasurable. Christians, by seeking God's will for their sex lives, should be able to experience the fulness of their glorious reunion.

Turning our eyes to the giver of the gift

As a pastor, I have had many opportunities to stand beside a groom while he awaits his bride's entrance. What a powerful moment this is! The groom stands facing the congregation. He is filled with the anticipation of catching even a glimpse of his beautiful bride. He waits and waits. He takes a deep breath. Then she steps out. He sees the first flash of her white wedding gown. Next the groom gains a full view of the radiant young woman adorned for him. The wedding march plays triumphantly, the congregation rises in honour of her approach, and she is brought before him and given to him. He then becomes united to her through covenant and he kisses her to demonstrate this union. He then takes her away to fully consummate the marriage and to begin a new life in which they will dwell together as long as they both shall live.

Human weddings and human sexuality are wonderful things, but do you realize that the purpose of them is to teach us about something so much greater? One cannot begin to ponder the gift of human love and sexuality without first turning to contemplate what this gift reveals about its giver. Human love and sexuality reveal something profound about our God and his relationship to his people. Have you considered that the 'one flesh' union of husband and wife gives us insight into our mystical union with our heavenly Bridegroom? Have you paused to consider that the yearning for consummation between a husband and wife is, at the very least, suggestive of how Christians should long for the Wedding Supper of the Lamb? Our sexuality, like all of God's gifts, should not lead us to focus on humanity, but rather it should turn our eyes to the giver of this gift. As you experience the temporal joys of glorious reunion with your spouse, contemplate how these earthly joys foreshadow heavenly realities. Think of the glories of the most important wedding:

> I saw the Holy City, the new Jerusalem, coming down out of heaven from God, prepared as a bride beautifully dressed for her husband. And I heard a loud voice from the throne saying, 'Now the dwelling of God is with men, and he will live with them. They will be his people, and God himself will be with them and be their God,'
>
> (Revelation 21:2-3).

Are you yearning for that day? Do you sense the anticipation and joy of it? Do you see how your glorious reunion with your spouse ultimately points to the most glorious reunion of all?

At the end of this age, the Christian, as part of the bride of Christ, will ultimately be reunited with his God in a fulness which will transcend that experienced by our first parents in the Garden of Eden. The most glorious reunion of all, which is foreshadowed by the earthly reunion experienced between husband and wife, is the believer's reunion with Jesus Christ.

Roger Ellsworth comments as follows on the exceeding joy of that great day:

> When the Lord Jesus finally takes to himself the people the Father gave him, not one will be missing. The bride will be complete. And she will not disappoint Christ. The Lord will not receive a bride spattered with the mud of iniquity and dressed in the tattered rags of sin. The plan of redemption will not produce a deficient church and a dejected Christ. It will rather yield to our Lord a complete bride who is perfectly fair. And the one who loved her, with a love surpassing comprehension, will be ecstatic over her.[18]

What a glorious day that will be! What a glorious reunion! Let your glorious reunion with your earthly spouse ever remind you of that coming great and glorious union with your heavenly spouse.

Questions for discussion and review

1. *Read the following texts and summarize what each teaches us about the nature of human sexuality:*

Text	Lesson
Genesis 1:28 and Genesis 4:1	_____
Genesis 2:24	_____
Genesis 24:67 and Deuteronomy 24:5	_____
1 Corinthians 7:2-5	_____

2. *Have you been open and honest with your fiancé or your spouse about your sexual history? Have you shared with them your sexual sins? Have you revealed to them things which might impact your sexual relationship including physical issues and issues such as sexual abuse etc.? If you are married, have you shared with your spouse the fulness of your sexual desire? Have you been honest about your sexual expectations, particularly regarding frequency? If you have failed to be fully open with your spouse about these matters make a commitment to do this immediately.*

3. *Read the following passages from the book of Proverbs and contemplate and discuss what they reveal about the dangers of sexual desire, particularly in men: Proverbs 5:1-23; 6:23-35; and 7:1-27. Discuss with your partner, and perhaps your pastor, how these dangers can be avoided through a healthy sex life within your marriage.*

4. *Read 1 Peter 3:7 and contemplate and discuss how this verse should direct the behaviour of husbands in the sexual relationship.*

5. *Read Philippians 2:3-4 and discuss how this applies to the sexual aspect of the marital relationship.*

11. The final note:
awaiting the crescendo

'For the creation was subjected to frustration, not by its own choice, but by the will of the one who subjected it, in hope that the creation itself will be liberated from its bondage to decay and brought into the glorious freedom of the children of God. We know that the whole creation has been groaning as in the pains of childbirth right up to the present time. Not only so, but we ourselves, who have the firstfruits of the Spirit, groan inwardly as we wait eagerly for our adoption as sons, the redemption of our bodies. For in this hope we were saved. But hope that is seen is no hope at all. Who hopes for what he already has? But if we hope for what we do not yet have, we wait for it patiently,'
(Romans 8:20-25).

'Come away, my lover, and be like a gazelle or like a young stag on the spice-laden mountains,'
(Song 8:14).

What the Bible teaches about marriage

'He who testifies to these things says, "Yes, I am coming soon."
Amen. Come, Lord Jesus,'
(Revelation 22:20).

In the film *The Wizard of Oz* a young girl named Dorothy becomes disenchanted with life in Kansas. Dorothy longs to find a better place, a different world. She subsequently finds herself in the midst of a violent tornado and she is knocked unconscious. She then enters the strange fantasy land of Oz. She has realized her desire for a different world. However, Dorothy quickly realizes how wonderful life in Kansas really was and she begins a quest to return home. Eventually, after much travail, she is able to return to Kansas. The film concludes with Dorothy declaring, 'There's no place like home.'

In some ways, *The Wizard of Oz* parallels the grand story of redemptive history as it is revealed in the Bible. Like Dorothy, Adam and Eve began to think there was a better world out there, a world in which they could be like God and possess the knowledge of good and evil. Again, like Dorothy, Adam and Eve realized their longing, and found themselves in a new world; but they too quickly discovered that it was far from a better world. In the Garden of Eden, Adam and Eve lived in perfect harmony with one another. There was no enmity between husband and wife. In the Garden of Eden, Adam and Eve experienced true sexual liberation and joy, they were 'both naked, and they felt no shame' (Genesis 2:25). Outside of Eden, however, Adam and Eve experienced marital disharmony ('Your desire will be for your husband, and he will rule over you', Genesis 3:16) and shame regarding their nakedness ('The LORD God made garments of skin for Adam and his wife and clothed them', Genesis 3:21). One cannot help but imagine that as Adam and Eve journeyed east of Eden they were longing for home. However, if they did indeed turn their eyes longingly back to Eden what they would have seen was that the garden was now guarded by cherubim to prevent their re-entry (Genesis 3:24). Unlike Dorothy, Adam and Eve could never go home again ... or could they?

Back to the beginning

In this book we have examined how to prepare for, how to define and how to maintain true love. In nearly every chapter there has been some reference or allusion to the first three chapters of Genesis. Why have we continually gone back to the beginning? It is because these three chapters of Genesis are foundational to understanding God's purpose for marriage and sexuality. We must go back to the beginning in order to understand who we are meant to be as husbands and wives. In some sense, this book is an effort to return home. We have, as it were, been knocking on Eden's door. We have been longing for home. However, we are not alone in our desire to return to the marital bliss of the Garden of Eden. The author of the Song of Songs, and the couple in the Song, also desire to go home again.

The human author of the Song of Songs reveals this desire to return to the Garden of Eden, to return home, by drawing significantly on the imagery of the early chapters of Genesis. The thematic parallels between the Song of Songs and the early chapters of Genesis are so powerful that it is undeniable that the author, under inspiration of the Holy Spirit, was making these connections purposefully. By means of these parallels the author of the Song of Songs holds out the hope of the redemptive power of God. He tells us that married couples can, through Jesus Christ, return to the garden. The Song of Songs reveals that we can once again return home. Let's look at how the author of the Song reaches back to the beginning and connects the story of the lovers in the Song to the story of the first lovers.

A return to the garden

One of the most direct and overt connections between the Song of Songs and the early chapters of Genesis is that both use the imagery of a garden. The book of Genesis begins with a man and woman in love and in a garden. The Song of Songs echoes this pattern. For example, consider the following verses from the Song of Songs:

4:12-14: 'You are a *garden* locked up, my sister, my bride; you are a spring enclosed, a sealed fountain. Your plants are an orchard of pomegranates with choice fruits, with henna and nard, nard and saffron, calamus and cinnamon, with every kind of incense tree, with myrrh and aloes and all the finest spices,' (emphasis mine).[1]

4:15-16: 'You are a *garden* fountain, a well of flowing water streaming down from Lebanon. Awake, north wind, and come, south wind! Blow on my *garden*, that its fragrance may spread abroad. Let my lover come into his *garden* and taste its choice fruits,' (emphasis mine).

5:1: 'I have come into my *garden*, my sister, my bride; I have gathered my myrrh with my spice. I have eaten my honeycomb and my honey; I have drunk my wine and my milk. Eat, O friends, and drink; drink your fill, O lovers,' (emphasis mine).

6:2: 'My lover has gone down to his *garden*, to the beds of spices, to browse in the *gardens* and to gather lilies,' (emphasis mine).

8:13: 'You who dwell in the *gardens* with friends in attendance, let me hear your voice!' (emphasis mine).[2]

This use of the garden imagery is deliberate on the part of the author of the Song of Songs. He wants his readers to recall the bliss of the Garden of Eden. He wants them to yearn for home and he tells them that it is possible to return there.

I began this book by referring to Genesis 2:25: 'The man and his wife were both naked, and they felt no shame.' In the Garden of Eden, Adam and Eve experienced romantic marital love without sin or shame. The Song of Songs tells us, by means of this garden imagery, that this can be experienced once again. As Raymond Dillard and Tremper Longman note, 'When we turn to the Song of Songs, we see the man and his wife in the garden naked and feeling anything but shame! ... The book pictures the restoration of human love to its pre-Fall bliss.'[3] The Song of Songs reminds us that Christians can once again experience love and sexuality without sin and without

211

shame. The Song reveals that married couples can return to the garden. We can go home again.

A new desire

A second connection between the Song of Songs and the early chapters of Genesis is that the couple in the Song have eradicated the enmity between male and female which was part of the curse of the Fall. After the Fall, God declared to the woman, in the presence of the man, the following curse: 'I will greatly increase your pains in childbearing; with pain you will give birth to children. *Your desire will be for your husband, and he will rule over you,*' (Genesis 3:16, emphasis mine). Inherent in this curse is the idea that husbands and wives, as a result of the Fall, will be in conflict with one another. According to this curse, the 'desire' of wives will be to dominate their husbands, but, ironically, instead they will be dominated *by* their husbands ('he will rule over you'). The desire spoken of in Genesis 3:16 is not a holy desire or a 'good' desire. It is the desire of domination and manipulation. This verse pictures a power struggle between husbands and wives. As Derek Kidner notes in his comments on Genesis 3:16: 'to love and cherish' becomes 'to desire and dominate'.[4]

In contrast, however, the Song displays a husband and wife reversing

> The Song of Songs reminds us that Christians can once again experience love and sexuality without sin and without shame.

this sinful pattern. The couple in the Song live in harmony and peace. There is no abuse of authority on the part of the husband, but rather he leads his wife with loving care. Similarly, the wife in the Song is not a radical feminist desiring to assert her dominance over her husband, but rather she lovingly submits to him. In essence, the Song reveals that redeemed couples can overcome the enmity of the curse, they can reverse it. In fact, some commentators contend that the Song includes a direct, intentional and overt reversal of the curse found in Genesis 3:16. Let me explain.

In Genesis 3:16 we learn that part of the curse is that a wife's 'desire' will be for her husband. We have seen that this means that she will desire to dominate her husband. However, in Song 7:10 we learn that it is the husband who now desires his wife. In that verse, the woman declares, 'I belong to my lover, and his *desire* is for me,' (emphasis mine). Here we see a direct reversal of the curse of Genesis 3:16. Andreas Köstenberger explains the nature of the reversal:

> Rather than the woman's desire being illegitimately to control her husband, a restoration of the original state is envisioned in which the husband's desire will be for his wife. Once again the woman gladly rests in the assurance that she is her husband's, and the husband does not dominate his wife but desires her.[5]

Commentator Richard Hess expresses the essence of the reversal this way: '...the Genesis judgment of each person seeking domination is reversed, with each person now seeking mutuality and willingly giving possession of their body to their partner'.[6] The Song of Songs reveals that the sinful domination which so often plagues the marital relationship can be exchanged for a new loving desire. It tells us we can go home again.

From murder to love

A third connection between the Song of Songs and the early chapters of Genesis is an interesting parallel which exists between Song 7:11 and Genesis 4:8. In Song 7:11, after the woman mentions that her husband's desire is for her, she invites her husband out to the countryside for a romantic encounter: 'Come, my lover, *let us go to the countryside*, let us spend the night in the villages,' (emphasis mine). In Genesis 4, after God reveals that sin desires to rule and dominate Cain, Cain invites his brother Abel out into the countryside to murder him: 'Now Cain said to his brother Abel, *"Let's go out to the field."* And while they were in the field, Cain attacked his brother Abel and killed him,' (Genesis 4:8, emphasis mine).[7] Both texts use the word 'desire'[8] and both texts include an invitation to the countryside. However, in the case of Genesis 4, Cain uses this encounter as an opportunity to murder his brother (in other words, sin triumphs), whereas in the account of Song 7:11, the woman uses this encounter to share love with her husband (in other words, love triumphs).

Once again the Song reveals a reversal of the curse. Murder is replaced by love. The Song tells us we can return home again.

Our only way home

These thematic parallels between the Song of Songs and Genesis clearly suggest that the intention of the author of the Song was to give us a road map home. The Song provides us with guideposts which point us in the direction of the Garden of Eden. It provides us with a portrait of redeemed human love and sexuality. However, it reminds us that we cannot return home in our own power. As we have seen, the Song is not naive about the continuing power and presence of sin. It warns us against the perversion of love. It tells us we are subject to awakening love at the wrong times and it reminds us that we, like Solomon, are prone to cheapen love. So how did the sinful couple of the Song find their way home? How did they overcome their own sinfulness? They did it the same way we do it, through the redemptive work of Jesus Christ. The Song, by continually pointing to divine love, reminds us that Jesus Christ is our only way home.

Jesus Christ has reversed the curse in every realm of this world, including the sphere of human sexuality and marital relations. Through the redemptive power of Christ, murder gives way to love, enmity gives way to harmony and sinful domination gives way to holy desire. The curses of the Fall which impact the marital relationship have been reversed by Jesus Christ and because of this Christian couples

> **Jesus Christ has reversed the curse in every realm of this world, including the sphere of human sexuality and marital relations.**

can have great hope that their marriages can be redeemed as well. Christ can redeem and restore your relationship. What a glorious truth! Through Christ, Christian couples can return to the bliss of the garden. We can once again go home.

However, the good news gets even better for Christians. The redemptive power of Christ not only allows couples to return to the garden, but it also allows them to transcend the glories of that garden. For Christianity does not ultimately look back, but rather looks forward. In the book of Revelation, the apostle John describes the New Jerusalem by making a variety of allusions to the Garden of Eden, but he also informs us that the end will be even more glorious than the beginning.[9] Vern Poythress notes the following regarding the relationship between the New Jerusalem and the Garden of Eden, 'But the apex of history is ever so much more magnificent than the beginning. The garden is now also a city, and the light has completely driven out the night.'[10] Our ultimate destination, our true home, is not a garden, but a holy city! A place prepared for us by our bridegroom, the risen Christ! Our ultimate destination is a place even more glorious than the Garden of Eden. The Song reminds us that we can go home again, and what a glorious home it will be!

A good marriage is not enough

The greatest benefit of the Song of Songs is not that it teaches us about romance and relationships, but that it points us to the necessity of the redeeming work of Christ in our lives. In essence, the Song reminds us that the purpose of romance and sexuality is to drive us to the Saviour. C. S. Lewis described human pain and suffering as God's 'megaphone'. His point was that pain and suffering should get our attention and lead us to God. Human romance and sexuality may also be used by God to attract our attention and lead us to him.[11] As Richard Hess notes, '...sex enables an experience of love whose intensity has no parallel in this cosmos and serves as a signpost to point to the greater love that lies beyond it'.[12] So while the Song takes us back to the Garden of Eden it also thrusts our hearts and minds forward to the fulness of redemption found in the new heavens and the new earth. If you miss this point you miss the ultimate message of the Song.

In the end, the purpose of the Song of Songs is to point us to *the* consummation and to *the* greatest love of all. As this book comes to its close, I want to leave you with this last crucial thought: a good marriage is not enough. In fact, marriage itself is not enough. In order to find true happiness, in order to experience ultimate bliss, in order to truly go home again, you must, like Tolkien declared, go 'beyond the walls of the world'. You must go to a place where people will 'neither marry nor be given in marriage' (Matthew 22:30). In other words, human love will never satisfy your ultimate longings. Human love is not an end in itself; it is simply a signpost to something so much greater. As Cornelius Plantinga Jr so aptly notes:

> Even if we fall deeply in love and marry another human being, we discover that our spiritual and sexual oneness isn't final. It's wonderful, but not final. It might even be as good as human oneness can be, but something in us keeps saying 'not this' or 'still beyond'.[13]

Plantinga concludes by noting, 'The truth is nothing in this earth can finally satisfy us. Much can make us content for a time, but nothing can fill us to the brim.'[14] Despite all of our culture's romantic notions regarding human love, the Bible tells us that only Jesus can fill us to the brim. Therefore, like the entire creation, we groan in anticipation, yearning and longing for our true home where we will dwell with our eternal spouse and experience perfect love. As the apostle Paul put it in his letter to the Romans: 'we hope for what we do not yet have' and 'we wait for it patiently' (Romans 8:25). We await, with bated breath, the great crescendo.

After reflecting on the Song of Songs, a book of poems regarding human love, I leave you with a poem which draws its imagery from the Song of Songs and which points us to the greatest love of all:

The weary pilgrim now at rest

A pilgrim I on earth, perplexed
With sins, with cares and sorrows vexed,
By age and pains brought to decay,
And my clay house mould'ring away.
Oh! How I long to be at rest
And soar on high among the blest!
This body shall in silence sleep;
Mine eyes no more shall ever weep;
No fainting fits shall me assail,
Nor grinding pains, my body frail;
With cares and fears ne'er cumbered be,
Nor losses know, nor sorrows see.

What though my flesh shall there consume?
It is the bed Christ did perfume;
And when a few years shall be gone,
This mortal shall be clothed upon;
A corrupt carcass down it lies,
A glorious body it shall rise;
In weakness and dishonor sown,
In power 'tis raised by Christ alone.
Then soul and body shall unite
And of their maker have the sight,
Such lasting joys shall there behold
As ear ne'er heard nor tongues e'er told.
Lord, make me ready for the day!
Then come, dear bridegroom, come away!

(Anne Bradstreet)

♦ ♦ ♦ ♦

'The Spirit and the bride say, "Come!" And let him who hears say, "Come!" Whoever is thirsty, let him come; and whoever wishes, let him take the free gift of the water of life'
(Revelation 22:17).

Questions for discussion and review

1. *Discuss with your spouse whether you think your marriage is headed in the right direction. Ask one another whether you are committed to cultivating a marriage which reflects the bliss of the garden, the joy of the Song of Songs and the redemptive glory of Jesus Christ.*

2. *Discuss the matter of 'desire' with your spouse. Ask yourself if your desire for your spouse reflects the spirit of Genesis 3:16 or Song of Songs 7:10.*
3. *Read Genesis 1-2 and Revelation 22. Make a list of the thematic connections between these two sections of Scripture.*
4. *List and discuss the ways in which human love and sexuality act like a megaphone calling us to God.*
5. *Review the chapters of this book and discuss with your spouse what you have learned. Make specific commitments to work on various areas of your marriage.*

Epilogue

I can recall my first encounter with the Song of Songs as a new Christian. I thought to myself, 'What is a book like this doing in the Bible?' Perhaps you have asked yourself the same question. My hope is that after the journey through this book you now have a grasp of why this book is in the Bible. My goal has been to demonstrate that the Song of Songs provides Christians with the wisdom necessary to guide them in the areas of marriage, romance and sexuality. Now that you have read and contemplated the Song of Songs, my hope is that instead of asking 'What is a book like this doing in the Bible?' you will ask 'What if this book wasn't in the Bible?' My point is that the Song of Songs provides us with insights which we do not find in other parts of Scripture. Tremper Longman put it this way: 'In answer to the question, "What is a book like the Song of Songs doing in the canon?" we respond by asking the reader to imagine the Bible without the Song. Without the Song, the church and synagogue would be left with spare and virtually exclusively negative words about an important aspect of our lives. Sexuality is a major aspect of the human experience, and God in his wisdom has spoken through the poet(s) of the Song to encourage us as well as warn us about its power in our lives.'[1] I hope that by reading this book you have grown in your appreciation of the Song of Songs, that it has enriched your marriage, and most importantly of all, that it has taught you about the incredible love of God revealed in Jesus Christ, 'For God so loved the world that he gave his one and only Son, that whoever believes in him shall not perish but have eternal life,' (John 3:16).

Notes

Chapter 1

1. This book is also known as the 'Song of Solomon'. For a helpful discussion of issues such as the title and authorship of the Song of Songs see Raymond B. Dillard's and Tremper Longman's *An Introduction to the Old Testament* (Grand Rapids, MI: Zondervan, 1994), pp.257-265.
2. For a detailed discussion of the interpretative issues regarding the Song of Songs see Tremper Longman's *Song of Songs: NICOT* (Grand Rapids, MI: Eerdmans, 2001), pp.1-70. For a helpful and exhaustive bibliography of resources on the Song of Songs see pages 70-83 of the same volume.
3. As found in Philip H. Eveson's foreword to Roger Ellsworth's *He is Altogether Lovely: Discovering Christ in the Song of Solomon* (Durham, England: Evangelical Press, 1998), p.10.

Chapter 2

1. Charles Spurgeon, *The Most Holy Place* (Pasadena, CA: Pilgrim Publishing, 1974), p.89.

2. Some commentators have mistakenly interpreted this verse as a request on the part of the couple not to be disturbed during physical intimacy. This interpretation is not supported by the text or the context and is rejected by most scholars.

3. Richard S. Hess, *Song of Songs*, Baker Commentary on the Old Testament (Grand Rapids, MI: Baker Academic, 2005), p.83.

4. Tremper Longman, *Song of Songs: NICOT* (Grand Rapids, MI: Eerdmans, 2001), pp.115-116.

5. O. Palmer Robertson, *The Genesis of Sex* (Phillipsburg, NJ: P & R, 2002), p.27.

6. Douglas Wilson, *Her Hand in Marriage* (Moscow, ID: Canon Press, 1997), pp.10-11. Author's note: While I have serious concerns regarding the theology of Douglas Wilson, particularly in the area of the doctrine of justification, I do find many of his insights on courtship and marriage both helpful and biblically sound.

7. As above, p.11.

8. As above, p.11.

9. Leslie Ludy, *Authentic Beauty* (Sisters, Oregon, Multnomah Publishers, Inc., 2003), p.120.

10. These qualities are obviously connected to the roles which husbands and wives are called to fulfil in the marriage relationship. At this point I just want to mention these qualities. I will discuss the issue of roles more fully in chapter eight.

Chapter 3

1. Gil Reavill, 'Tragedy of the Commons', *American Conservative*, 4 July 2005, p.9.

2. It is important to keep in mind that the concept of ancient betrothal is very different from the modern concept of marital engagement. Betrothal was a much more serious commitment than engagement is today. It carried many of the obligations and responsibilities of marriage.

3. Tom Gledhill, *The Message of the Song of Songs* (Downers Grove, IL: Inter-Varsity Press, 1994), p.129.

4. Douglas Wilson, *Her Hand in Marriage* (Moscow, ID: Canon Press, 1997), p.11.

5. O. Palmer Robertson, *The Genesis of Sex* (Phillipsburg, NJ: P & R, 2002), pp.97-98.

6. As above, p.101.

7. As above, p.101.

8. As above, p.101.

9. As above, p.101.

10. There is another statement of the woman's decision to be sexually pure in Song of Songs 4:12 where she is referred to lovingly by the man as a 'garden locked up', 'spring enclosed' and a 'sealed fountain'.

11. Gledhill is referring to Jesus' words in Matthew 5:29-30.

12. Gledhill, *The Message of the Song of Songs*, p.129.

Chapter 4

1. Robert Davidson, *Ecclesiastes and the Song of Solomon* (Louisville, KY: Westminster John Knox Press, 1986), p.151.

2. Richard S. Hess, *Song of Songs*, p.238.

3. Most commentators believe that the word 'arm' in verse 6 is likely a poetic synonym for 'finger'. Thus 'arm' is a reference to the signet ring which was worn on the finger.

4. Longman, *Song of Songs: NICOT*, p.210.

5. As above, p.210.

6. Palmer Robertson, *The Genesis of Sex*, p.32.

7. As above, pp.32-35.

8. As above, p.35.

9. Jay Adams, *Christian Living in the Home* (Phillipsburg, NJ: P &R, 1972), pp.52-53.

10. As above, p.52.

11. As above, p.53.

12. For those who think this promise is solely applied to the Old Testament nation of Israel, remember that Paul refers to the New Covenant church as the 'Israel of God' in Galatians 6:16.

Chapter 5

1. Gledhill, *The Message of the Song of Songs,* p.231.
2. As above, p.231.
3. Ian Provan, *Ecclesiastes/Song of Songs: The NIV Application Commentary* (Grand Rapids, MI: Zondervan, 2001), p.369.
4. Charles Hodge, *1 & 2 Corinthians: Geneva Series of Commentaries* (Carlisle, PA: Banner of Truth, reprinted 1994), pp.627-628.
5. Gledhill, *The Message of the Song of Songs*, pp.231-232.
6. Some biblical scholars claim that the name of God appears in this verse, that the flames being described here are actually the 'flames of Yahweh'. However, most scholars reject this suggestion, particularly because God's name is not present elsewhere in the Song. For more information on this issue see Tremper Longman, *Song of Songs: NICOT*, pp.212-213.
7. G. Lloyd Carr, *The Song of Solomon: Tyndale Old Testament Commentaries*, ed. D. J. Wiseman (Downers Grove, IL: Inter-Varsity Press, 1984), p.171.
8. Dan Doriani, *The Life of a God-Made Man* (Wheaton, IL: Crossway, 2001).
9. As above, p.57.

Chapter 6

1. It should be noted that the identity of the speaker in this verse is much disputed. Some commentators suggest the man is speaking while others suggest that it is the woman. Obviously, I have chosen the latter theory. However, the essential meaning of the text remains unchanged regardless of who is speaking.

2. Some commentators suggest that Solomon's vineyard is actually a metaphor for his vast harem.

3. S. Craig Glickman, *A Song for Lovers* (Downers Grove, IL: IVP 1976), p.101.

4. Longman, *Song of Songs: NICOT,* p.219.

5. As above, p.219.

6. Brian J. Walsh and Sylvia C. Keesmaat, *Colossians Remixed* (Downers Grove, IL: IVP, 2004), p.160.

7. Michael Bentley, *Colossians and Philemon* (England: Evangelical Press, 2002), p.132.

8. Note that this text also teaches us that by engaging in sexual sin we are also, by means of our union with Christ, associating Christ with such sin (i.e. in some way joining Christ with a prostitute). This should be unthinkable for a Christian!

9. Charles Hodge, *1 & 2 Corinthians* (Carlisle, PA: Banner of Truth, 1994), p.105.

10. Sue Shellenbarger, 'Giving Credit Where It's Due: Men Do More Housework Than Women Think', *The Wall Street Journal,* May 19, 2005, p. D1.

11. Sue Shellenbarger, 'For Richer or for Poorer, but Only If We Have Separate Checking Accounts', *The Wall Street Journal,* February 24, 2005, p. D1.

12. Gledhill, *The Message of the Song of Songs,* p.242.

Chapter 7

1. Marva J. Dawn, *Sexual Character* (Grand Rapids, MI: Eerdmans, 1993), p.55.

2. Longman, *Song of Songs: NICOT*, p.151. It is important to note that the reference to his lover as 'sister' in no way implies incest.

3. Richard S. Hess, *Song of Songs*: Baker Commentary on the Old Testament (Grand Rapids, MI: Baker Academic, 2005), p.142.

4. Paige Patterson, *Song of Solomon* (Chicago, IL: Moody Press, 1986), p.93.
5. Dan Doriani, *The Life of a God-Made Man* (Wheaton, IL: Crossway, 2001), p.57.
6. As Derek Kidner notes in his commentary on Genesis, '...the woman is presented wholly as his partner and counterpart, nothing is yet said of her as childbearer. She is valued for herself alone.' Derek Kidner, *Genesis: Tyndale Old Testament Commentaries*, Gen. Ed. D. J. Wiseman (Downers Grove, IL: IVP, 1967), p.65.
7. Andreas J. Köstenberger, *God, Marriage and Family: Rebuilding the Biblical Foundation* (Wheaton, Illinois: Crossway, 2004), p.34.
8. Dawn, *Sexual Character*, p.55.
9. C. S. Lewis, *The Four Loves* (New York, NY: Harcourt Brace & Company, 1988), p.67. *Eros* is the Greek word from which we get our English word 'erotic'. *Eros* is a way of referring to sexual intimacy.
10. As above, pp.67-68.
11. As above, p.65.
12. R. C. Sproul, *The Intimate Marriage* (Wheaton, IL: Tyndale House, 1986), pp.16-17.
13. Hans Walter Wolff, *Anthropology of the Old Testament* (Philadelphia, PA: Fortress, 1973), p.160.
14. Roger Ellsworth, *He is Altogether Lovely: Discovering Christ in the Song of Solomon* (Durham, England: Evangelical Press, 1998), p.143.

Chapter 8

1. Anthony A. Hoekema, *Created in God's Image* (Grand Rapids, MI: Eerdmans, 1986), p.76.
2. As above, p.77.

3.   Andreas J. Köstenberger, *God, Marriage and Family: Rebuilding the Biblical Foundation* (Wheaton, Illinois: Crossway, 2004), p.37.

4.   As above, p.42.

5.   Athalya Brenner, *The Israelite Woman: Social Role and Literary Type in Biblical Narratives* (JSOT Press, 1985), pp.46-50.

6.   Gledhill, *The Message of the Song of Songs,* pp.251-252.

7.   *NIV Spirit of the Reformation Study Bible,* Richard L. Pratt Jr, Gen. Ed., (Grand Rapids, MI: Zondervan, 2003), p.1061.

8.   John Piper, 'A Vision of Complementarity: Manhood and Womanhood Defined According to the Bible', *Recovering Biblical Manhood and Womanhood,* eds. John Piper and Wayne Grudem (Wheaton, IL: Crossway, 1991), p.42.

9.   As above, p.35.

10. This may seem to contradict the teachings of the Song which often displays the woman taking the sexual initiative. However, Piper is not ruling this out by his proposition. In fact, he notes, 'The woman may initiate an interest in romance and may keep on initiating different steps along the way. But there is a difference. A feminine initiation is in effect an invitation for the man to do his kind of initiating.' That is entirely consistent with the female initiation present in the Song, where the woman calls the man to lead her sexually. See Piper, 'A Vision of Complementarity: Manhood and Womanhood Defined According to the Bible', p.40.

11. Piper, 'A Vision of Complementarity', pp.38-41.

12. Matthew Henry, *Matthew Henry's Commentary on the Whole Bible,* vol. 1 (Peabody, MA: Hendrickson, 1991), p.16.

13. Köstenberger, *God, Marriage and Family,* p 75.

14. Wayne Grudem, 'Wives Like Sarah and the Husbands Who Honor Them', *Recovering Biblical Manhood and Womanhood,* eds. John Piper and Wayne Grudem (Wheaton, IL: Crossway, 1991), p.196.

15. It is interesting to note that the metaphor of a tree and shade is used of the relationship between God and his people in Hosea 14:7: 'Men will dwell again in his shade.'
16. Köstenberger, *God, Marriage and Family*, p.37.

Chapter 9

1. For instance, the Song does not deal with conflict resolution. There are many other popular marriage counselling books which attempt to deal with these matters. For help with these issues see Adams, *Christian Living in the Home*, pp.25-42.
2. This argument was set forth by M. H. Pope in his article 'A Mare in Pharaoh's Chariotry', *BASOR* 200 (1970), pp.56-61, and is discussed by Tremper Longman in his commentary on the Song of Songs. See Tremper Longman, *Song of Songs: NICOT*, p.103.
3. He expresses a similar sentiment in Song 5:2 where he refers to her as his 'flawless one' and in Song 6:9 where he declares that she is his 'perfect one'.
4. Gledhill, *The Message of the Song of Songs*, p.118.
5. Dan B. Allender and Tremper Longman, *Intimate Allies* (Wheaton, IL: Tyndale House Publishers, 1995), p.97.
6. Dawn, *Sexual Character*, p.56.
7. Matthew Henry, *Matthew Henry's Commentary on the Whole Bible*, p.886.
8. Ellsworth, *He is Altogether Lovely: Discovering Christ in the Song of Solomon*, p.157.
9. As above, p.157.
10. Adams, *Christian Living in the Home*, p.38.

Chapter 10

1. John Stott, *Our Social & Sexual Revolution* (Grand Rapids, MI: Baker, 1999), p.197.

Notes

2. Leland Ryken, *Worldly Saints: The Puritans As They Really Were* (Grand Rapids, MI: Zondervan, 1986), pp.40-41.

3. As above, p.41.

4. As above.

5. As above, pp.45-46.

6. As above, p.44.

7. Some suggest that the speakers here are the unmarried friends of the woman (the 'Daughters of Jerusalem'), but I reject this because it seems totally inappropriate that these women would be observers of this private moment. Therefore, I believe these words are from the narrator of the poem who interjects at the centrepiece of this masterpiece to give his affirmation and blessing.

8. Gledhill, *The Message of the Song of Songs,* p.167.

9. As above, p.174.

10. See chapters on the prerequisites of true love for an exposition of this verse.

11. Dawn, *Sexual Character,* p.24.

12. Some scholars have contended that the Song of Songs is structured in what is known as a 'chiastic' pattern in which the middle of the book becomes the climax of the story. If this contention is correct, then the couple's sexual encounter, which occurs most clearly in Song 5:1, would be the indication of the consummation of their marriage and the pinnacle of the book. For more information see Andrew Hwang, 'New Structure of the Song of Songs', *Westminster Theological Journal,* vol. 65, no. 1: Spring 2003, pp.79-111; and David A. Dorsey, 'Literary Structuring in the Song of Songs', *Journal for the Study of the Old Testament* 46, 1990, pp.81-96.

13. Robert G. Gromacki, *Called to Be Saints: An Exposition of 1 Corinthians* (Grand Rapids, MI: Baker, 1977), p.88.

14. Leland Ryken, *Worldly Saints,* p.39.

15. Gil Reavill, 'Tragedy of the Commons', *American Conservative,* 4 July 2005, p.8.

16. Longman, *Song of Songs: NICOT,* p.158.
17. Dawn, *Sexual Character,* p.21.
18. Ellsworth, *He is Altogether Lovely,* pp.215-216.

Chapter 11

1. The word 'orchard' in this verse is the Hebrew word *'pardes'* which may be translated as 'paradise'.
2. There is actually another reference to the garden theme in Song of Songs 6:11, but the term used there is 'grove' and not 'garden', 'I went down to the grove of nut trees to look at the new growth in the valley, to see if the vines had budded or the pomegranates were in bloom.'
3. Raymond B. Dillard and Tremper Longman III, *An Introduction to the Old Testament* (Grand Rapids, MI: Zondervan, 1994), p.265.
4. Derek Kidner, *Genesis: Tyndale Old Testament Commentaries,* Gen. Ed. D. J. Wiseman (Downers Grove, IL: IVP, 1967), p.71.
5. Köstenberger, *God, Marriage and Family,* p.54. It is interesting to note that the Hebrew word translated in Song 7:10 as 'desire' appears only three times in the entire Bible. In addition to its appearance in Song 7:10 and Genesis 3:16, it also appears in Genesis 4:7 where God addresses Cain and his sacrifice, 'If you do what is right, will you not be accepted? But if you do not do what is right, sin is crouching at your door; it *desires* to have you, but you must master it,' (emphasis mine). Obviously, the two uses of the word 'desire' in Genesis have negative connotations. Therefore, the only positive use of this word occurs in Song 7:10. This is further evidence of a connection between the Song and Genesis and that one of the purposes of the Song is to demonstrate that the curse on the husband and wife relationship has been reversed by the redemptive work of God.
6. Richard S. Hess, *Song of Songs,* p.224.

7. For a helpful discussion of this parallel, see Ian Provan's *Ecclesiastes/Song of Songs: The NIV Application Commentary* (Grand Rapids, MI: Zondervan, 2001), pp.358-359.

8. As mentioned in a previous footnote, the word 'desire' only appears three times in the entire Bible, therefore the fact that these two texts use this infrequently employed word enhances the argument for a strong connection between them.

9. Some of the connections between the Garden of Eden and the New Jerusalem include God's intimate dwelling with his people, God's blessing on his people, and, most prominently, the reappearance of the Tree of Life and the removal of the curse (Revelation 22:1-5).

10. Vern S. Poythress, *The Returning King* (Phillipsburg, NJ: P & R, 2000), p.192.

11. Lewis makes this point in the very same quote in which he refers to pain as God's 'megaphone' by noting that God also 'whispers' to us in our pleasures. While pleasure's voice may be more subtle in tone, its message is no less powerful.

12. Hess, *Song of Songs*, p.35.

13. Cornelius Plantinga Jr, *Engaging God's World* (Grand Rapids, MI: Eerdmans, 2002), p.5.

14. As above, p.6.

Epilogue

1. Longman, *Song of Songs: NICOT*, p.59.

Other titles in this series...

What the Bible

teaches about

angels

ANGELS in movies, television shows, figurines, books, magazine articles and seminars — angels are everywhere!

This would seem to be very good news. After all, the Bible does have a lot to say about angels, mentioning them 273 times. Should we not welcome such widespread interest in a biblical topic?

Yet interest in a biblical topic is of no value if we are not biblical about the topic. All too often, the only connection between the current angel-mania and the Bible is the teaching that angels exist.

In this straightforward and easy-to-read book in the *What the Bible teaches about...* series Roger Ellsworth sets the record straight, putting the biblical view of angels in a clear and helpful way, dealing with such topics as what are the seraphim and cherubim, angels as ministering spirits, and the role of angels at the beginning and end of time. Above all, however, is his concern to drive us to the one the angels themselves adore — the Lord Jesus Christ.

Roger Ellsworth, Evangelical Press, 128 pages, ISBN-13 978-0-85234-617-4; ISBN 0-85234-617-4

What the Bible

teaches about

guidance

How can I know God's will for me? What does God want me to do? How can I know I am doing the right thing? The question of divine guidance is one that has always caused confusion among Christians. In this book Peter Bloomfield dispels the notion that there is just one perfect plan for our lives, and urges us to follow the Scriptures which provide all we need to live lives that are pleasing to our heavenly Father.

'Young Christians in particular should be given this book. It will spare them much anguish in trying to reach important decisions — What course of study should I take? Whom should I marry? Where should I buy a house? This book will be welcomed by many and widely used.'

Allan M. Harman
(Melbourne, Victoria)

Peter Bloomfield, Evangelical Press, 208 pages, ISBN-13 978-0-85234-611-2; ISBN 0-85234-611-5.

A wide range of Christian books is available from Evangelical Press. If you would like a free catalogue please write to us or contact us by e-mail. Alternatively, you can view the whole catalogue online at our web site:

www.evangelicalpress.org.

Evangelical Press
Faverdale North, Darlington, Co. Durham, DL3 0PH, England

e-mail: sales@evangelicalpress.org

Evangelical Press USA
P. O. Box 825, Webster, New York 14580, USA

e-mail: usa.sales@evangelicalpress.org